Little Presents from the Heart

Rose, Heart, Girl, Boy, Flower, Ribbon...
Instructions on page 9. Use Aida cloth.

Elegant Lady

Instructions on page 10. Use Aida cloth.

ABCDEFGHIJKL
MNOPQRSTUVW
XYZ:1234567890

Wonderful Bouquet

Instructions on page 11. Use Aida cloth.

Happy Circle

Instructions on page 12. Use Aida cloth.

# Greenery Town

Instructions on page 13. Use Aida cloth.

Garment Case
Toiletry Case
Tissue Case

These handy cases help keep you organized for your entire trip. Instructions on pages 47 and 48.

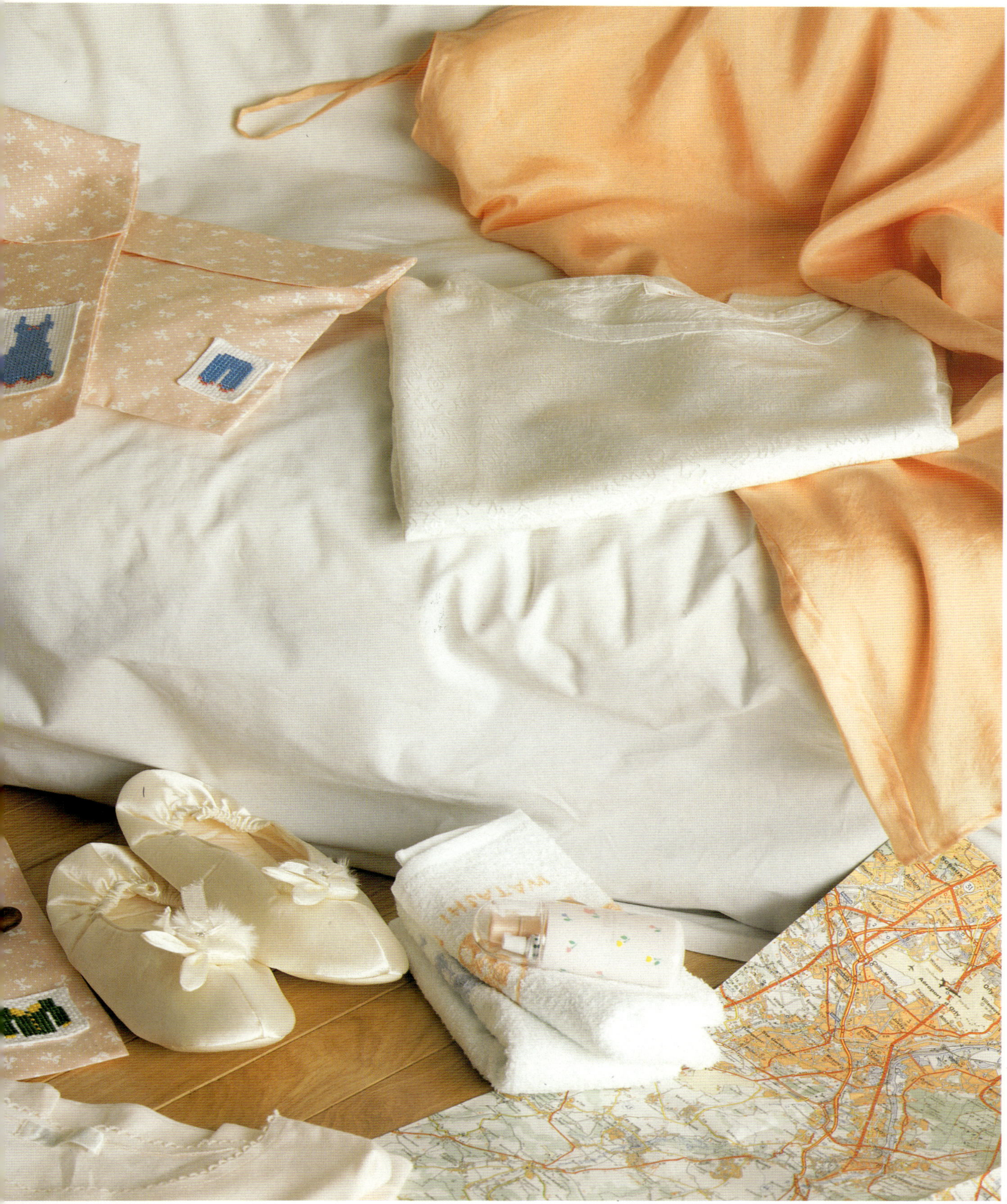

Pouch, Mini Sewing Case

Make lovely articles from remnant embroidery fabrics worked with simple designs.
You can make original name tapes, too.
Instructions on pages 49 and 50.

☆ Shown on page 1.

2-strand

Holbein stitch (700)

Holbein stitch (321)

● = 700   ○ = 321   ✕ = 603   △ = 948   ▲ = 938

Use DMC six-strand embroidery floss No. 25, shown by the color numbers, for all the designs in this book.

☆ Shown on page 2.

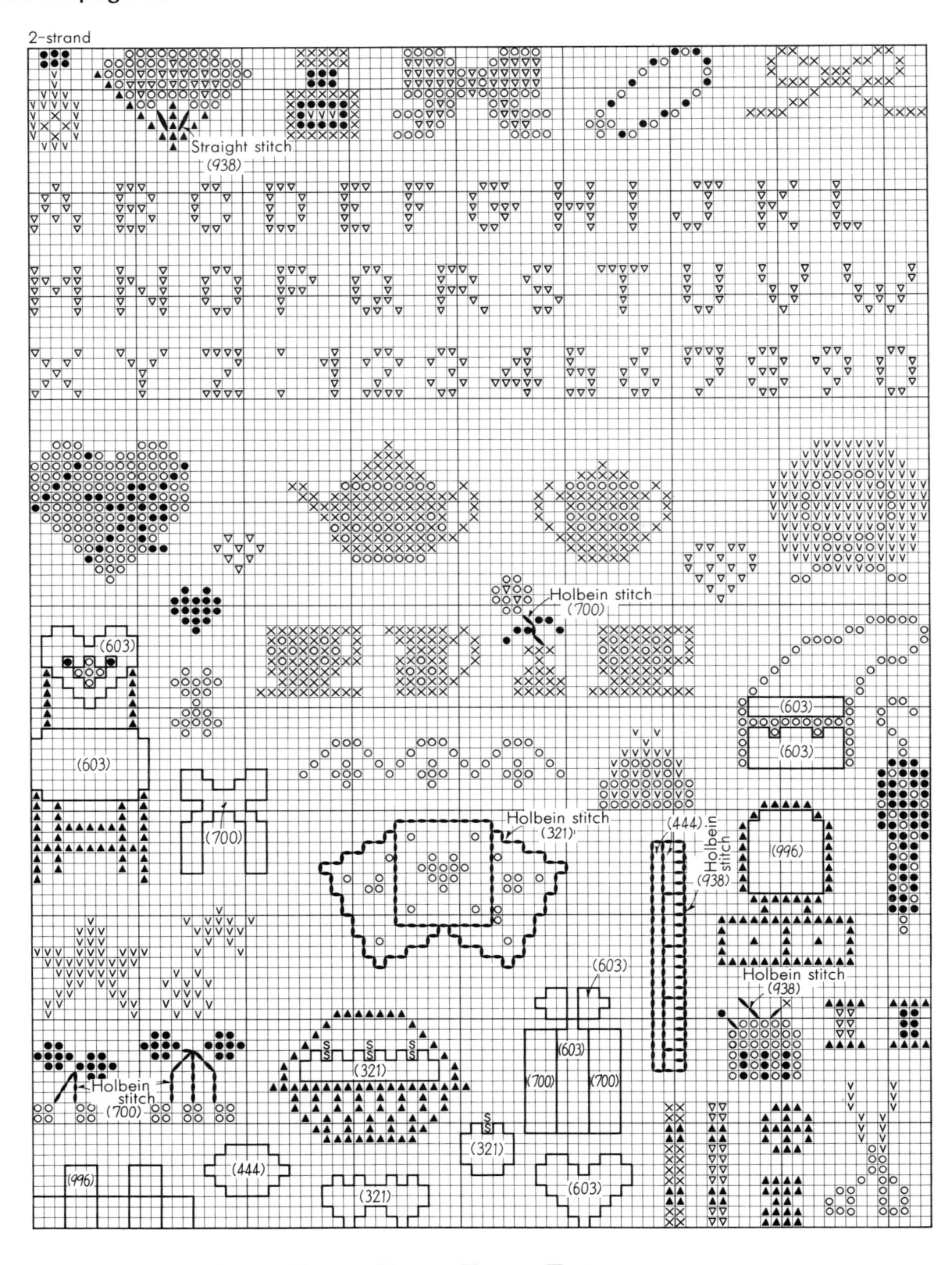

2-strand

● = 700   ○ = 321   ▽ = 603   ▲ = 938   ✕ = 996   V = 444   S = 890

☆ Shown on page 3.

2-strand

Holbein stitch (321)
Holbein stitch (890)
Holbein stitch (603)
Holbein stitch (321)
Holbein stitch (700)
Holbein stitch (890)
Straight stitch (890)

● = 700   ○ = 321   ▽ = 603   ✕ = 996   v = 444   S = 890   T = 333

☆ **Shown on page 4.**

2-strand

● = 700　◯ = 321　▽ = 603　• = 948　▲ = 938　□ = 996　V = 444　S = 890

☆ Shown on page 5.

2-strand

● = 700   ○ = 321   ▽ = 603   · = 948   ▲ = 938   ✕ = 996   ∨ = 444

13

☆**Shown on page 30.**

4-strand

EVERY DAY
NICE COOKING

Straight stitch (3363)

Straight stitch (839)

(350)

(350)

(350)

Straight stitch (3364)

(3363) (3363)

(350)

● =336   — =824   ○ =350   ▩ =927   △ =3363   ✕ =3364   ◣ =839   S =435

☆ Shown on page 31.

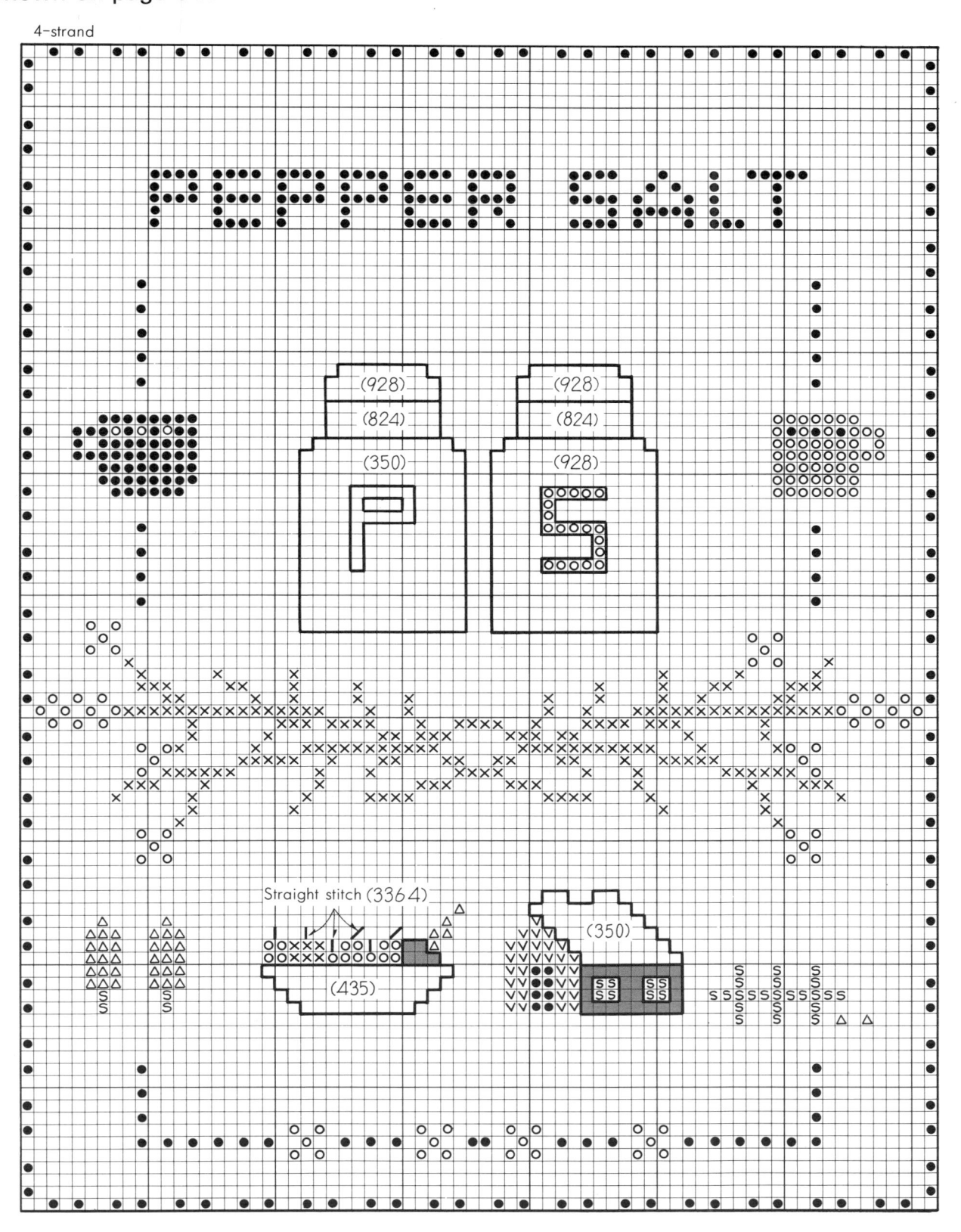

4-strand

● =336　◯ =350　□ =927　V= 928　△ =3363　X =3364　S = 435

☆ Shown on page 32.

3-strand

PLEASE HELP ME!

- Fly stitch (632)
- double wind French knot (632)
- Holbein stitch (666)
- single wind French knot (666)

Labels on chart: (452), (452), (738), (738), (738), (519), (738), (776), (738), (307), (353), (813), (813), (413), (775), (369), (452), (677)

○=666 ●=632 ·=3064 ▒=3345 ▽=3347 =452 ✕=312 ■=912 ▲=898 V=400 T=472

16

☆ Shown on page 33.
(666) 3-strand

single wind French knot

☆ Shown on page 34.

3-strand

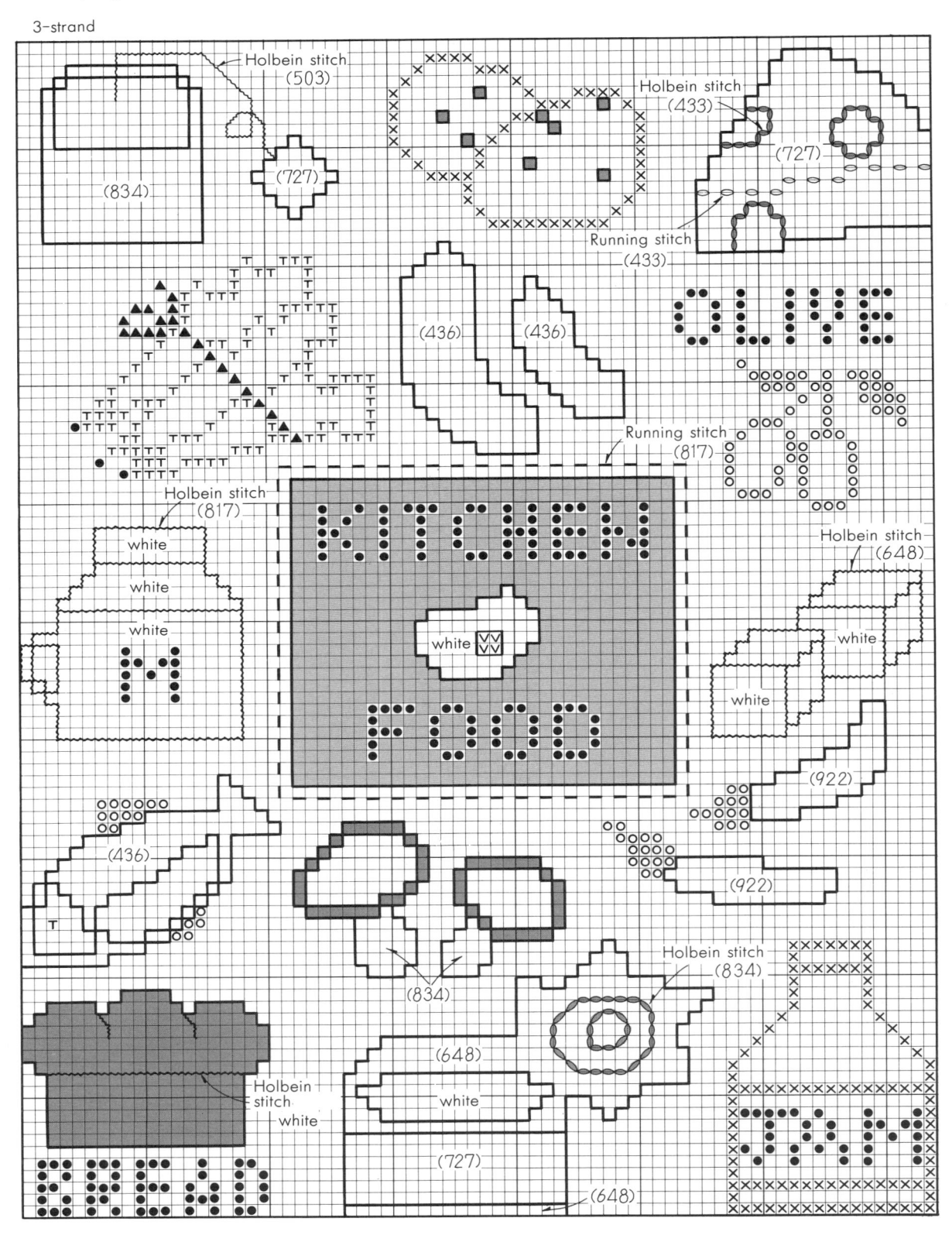

O = 503　V = 727　■ = 433　□ = 951　● = 817　T = 561　X = 3013　▲ = 834

☆ Shown on page 35.

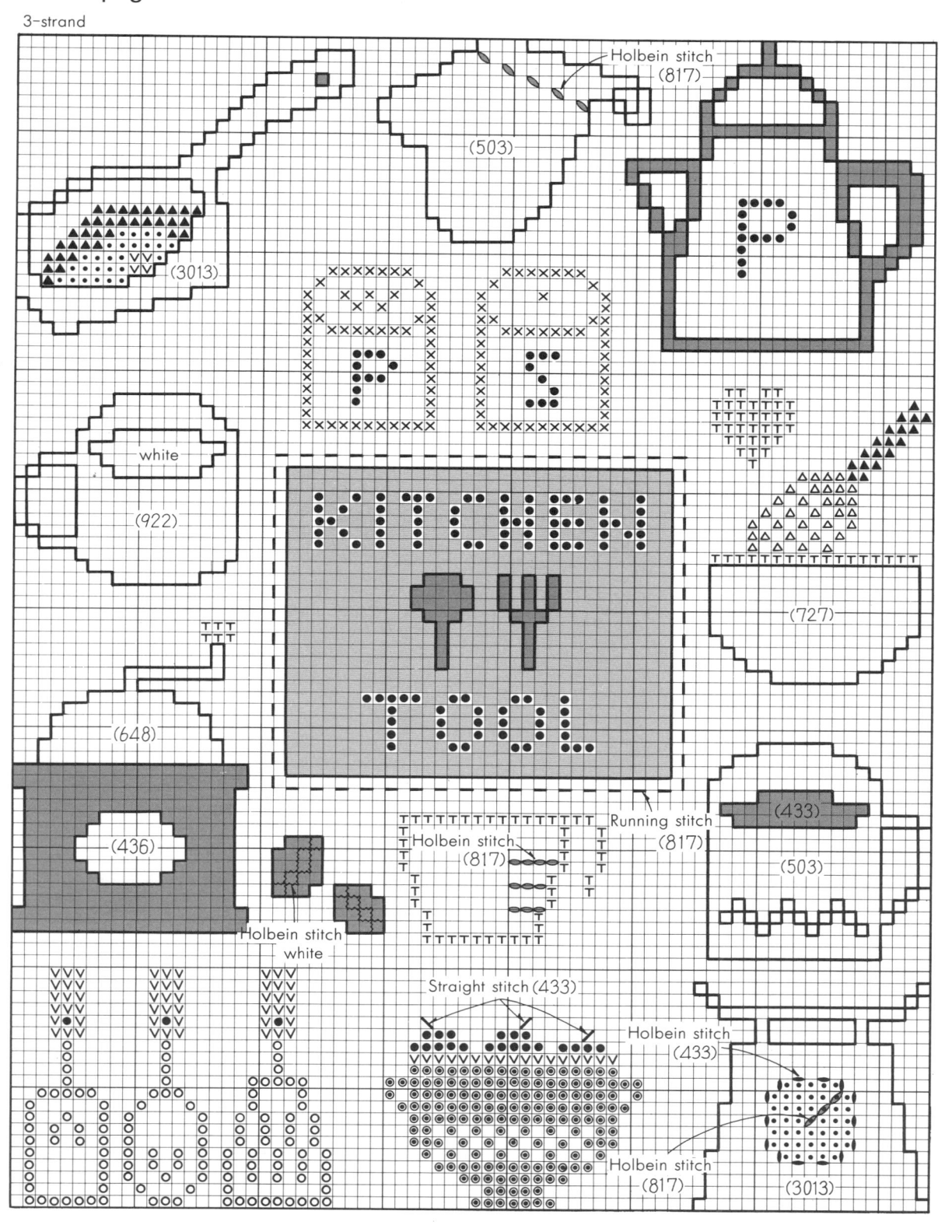

3-strand

○=503 V=727 ■=433 ▨=951 ●=817 T=561 X=3013 △=648 ▲=834 ⊙=436 •=white

☆ **Show on page 38.**

3-strand

good old days

● =434　○ =347　■ =470　▨ =422　△ =926　✕ =647　▲ =300

☆Shown on page 39.

3-strand unless otherwise specified.

■ = 931   ■ = 436   ● = 347   O = 422   ▲ = 433   △ = 223   ▽ = 783   S = 502   T = 898   U = 470   X = 3032

☆Shown on page 40.

3-strand unless otherwise sepcified.

■=336 □=666 ▲=910 ⊥=911 N=912 ☰=913 ●=825 ⊙=826 ▽=452 △=842 ✕=632 ◉=677 •=369
■=898 V=605 H=776 ∩=943 ╱=519

☆ Shown on page 41.

3-strand

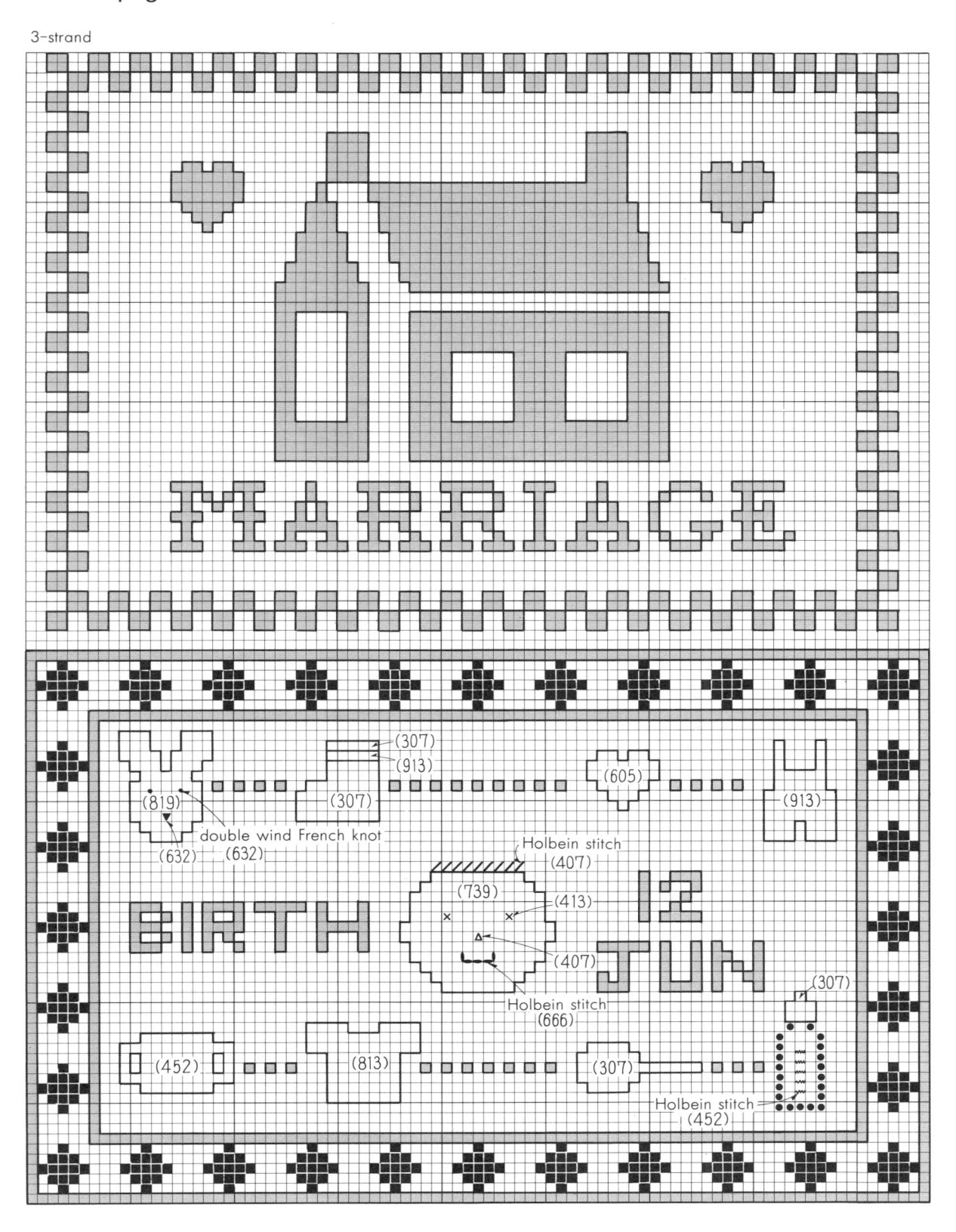

☆ Shown on page 66.

4-strand unless otherwise specified.

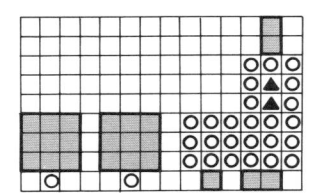

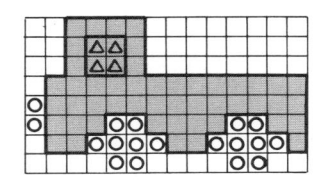

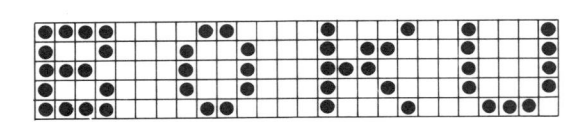

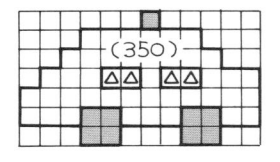

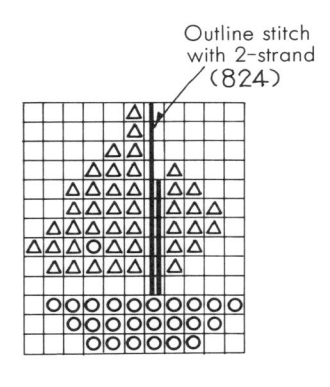

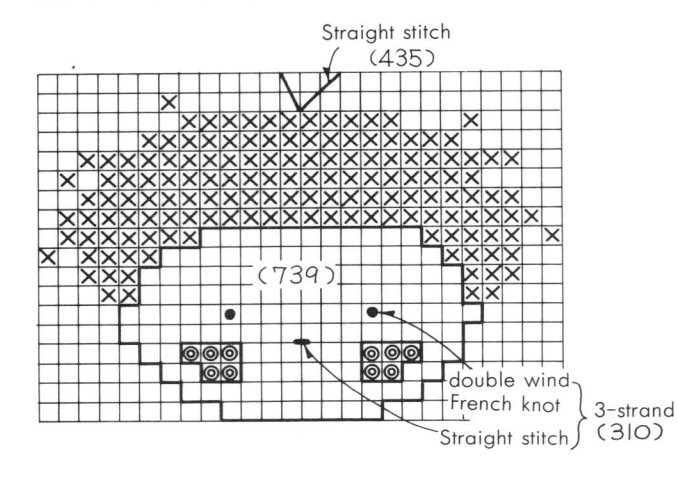

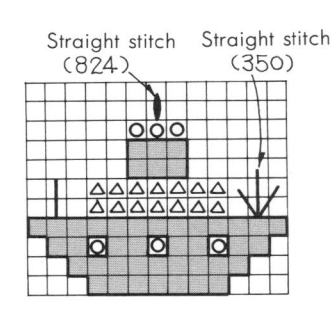

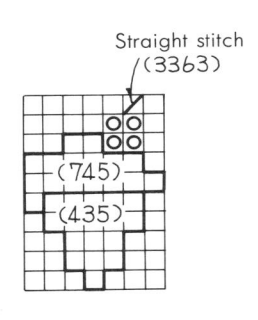

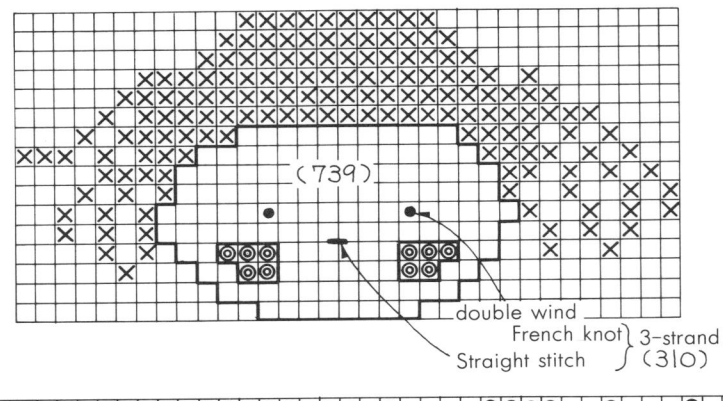

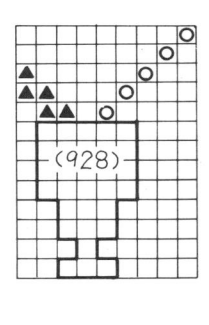

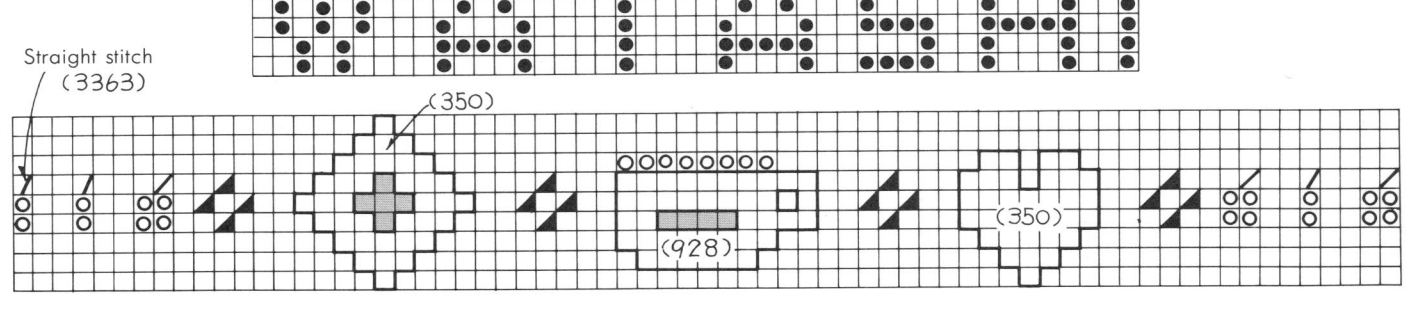

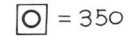

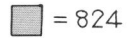

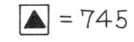

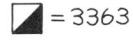

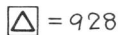

Outline stitch with 2-strand (824)

Straight stitch (435)

Straight stitch (824)   Straight stitch (350)

(739)

(350)

double wind French knot } 3-strand
Straight stitch } (310)

Straight stitch (3363)

(745)
(435)

(739)

(928)

double wind French knot } 3-strand
Straight stitch } (310)

Straight stitch (3363)

(350)

(928)

(350)

| ◯ = 350 | ▩ = 824 | ▲ = 745 | ◪ = 3363 | △ = 928 | ✕ = 435 | ● = 839 | ◎ = 758 |

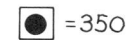

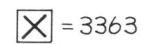

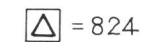

☆Shown on page 67.

4-strand unless otherwise specified.

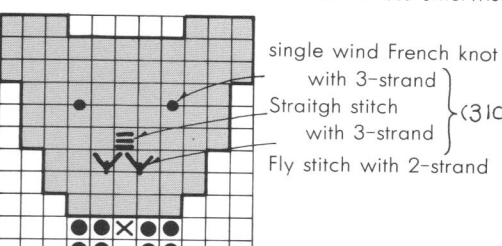

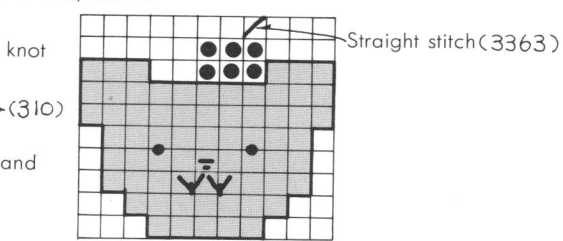

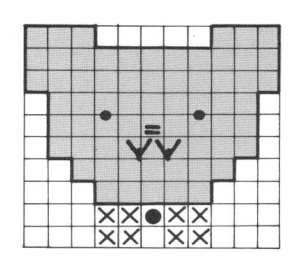

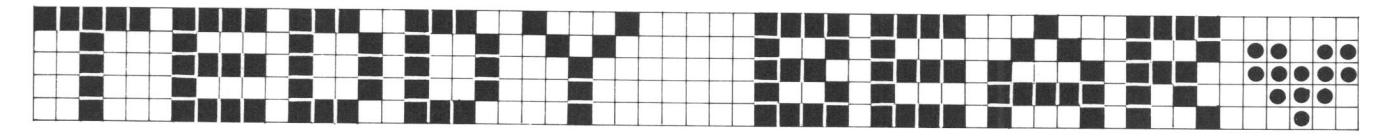

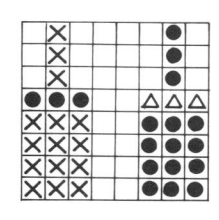

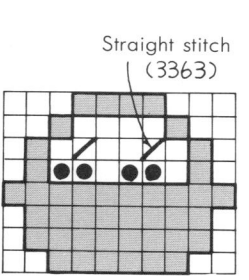

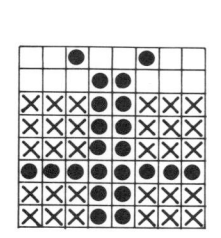

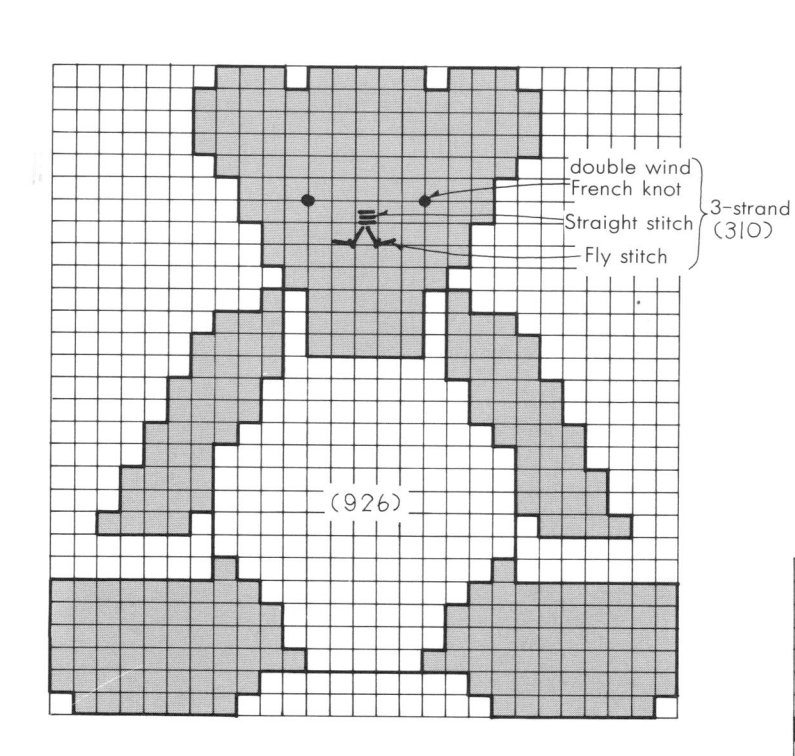

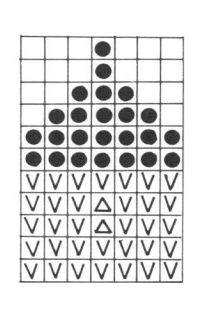

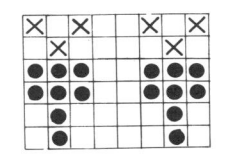

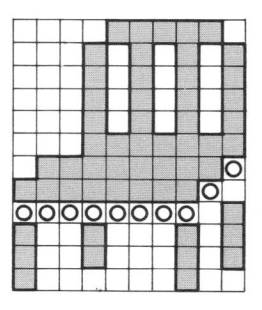

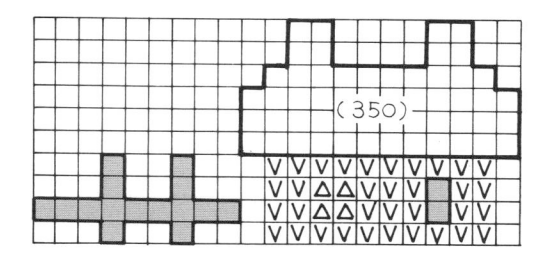

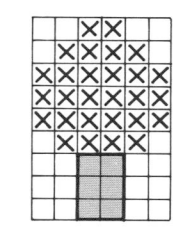

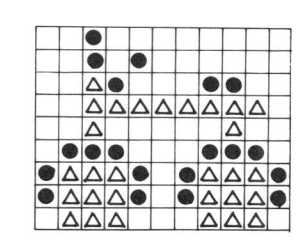

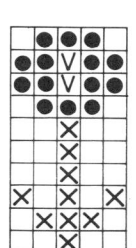

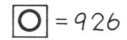

single wind French knot with 3-strand
Straitgh stitch with 3-strand } (310)
Fly stitch with 2-strand

Straight stitch (3363)

TEDDY BEAR

double wind French knot
Straight stitch } 3-strand (310)
Fly stitch

Straight stitch (3363)

(926)

(350)

▨ = 435   ◯ = 926   V = 928   ■ = 839   ● = 350   ✕ = 3363   △ = 824

☆Shown on page 68.

3-strand

■ =310　☒ =347　H =676　T =783　O =647　S =436　▓ =221　▒ =434　▲ =300　⊟ =422　△ =758　⊡ =712

☆ Shown on page 69.

● = 434　◯ = 3328　▧ = 436　▨ = 834　▲ = 347　△ = 926　S = 975　T = 640　U = 470　− = 502　∥ = 783　■ = 310　✕ = 976

☆Shown on page 29.

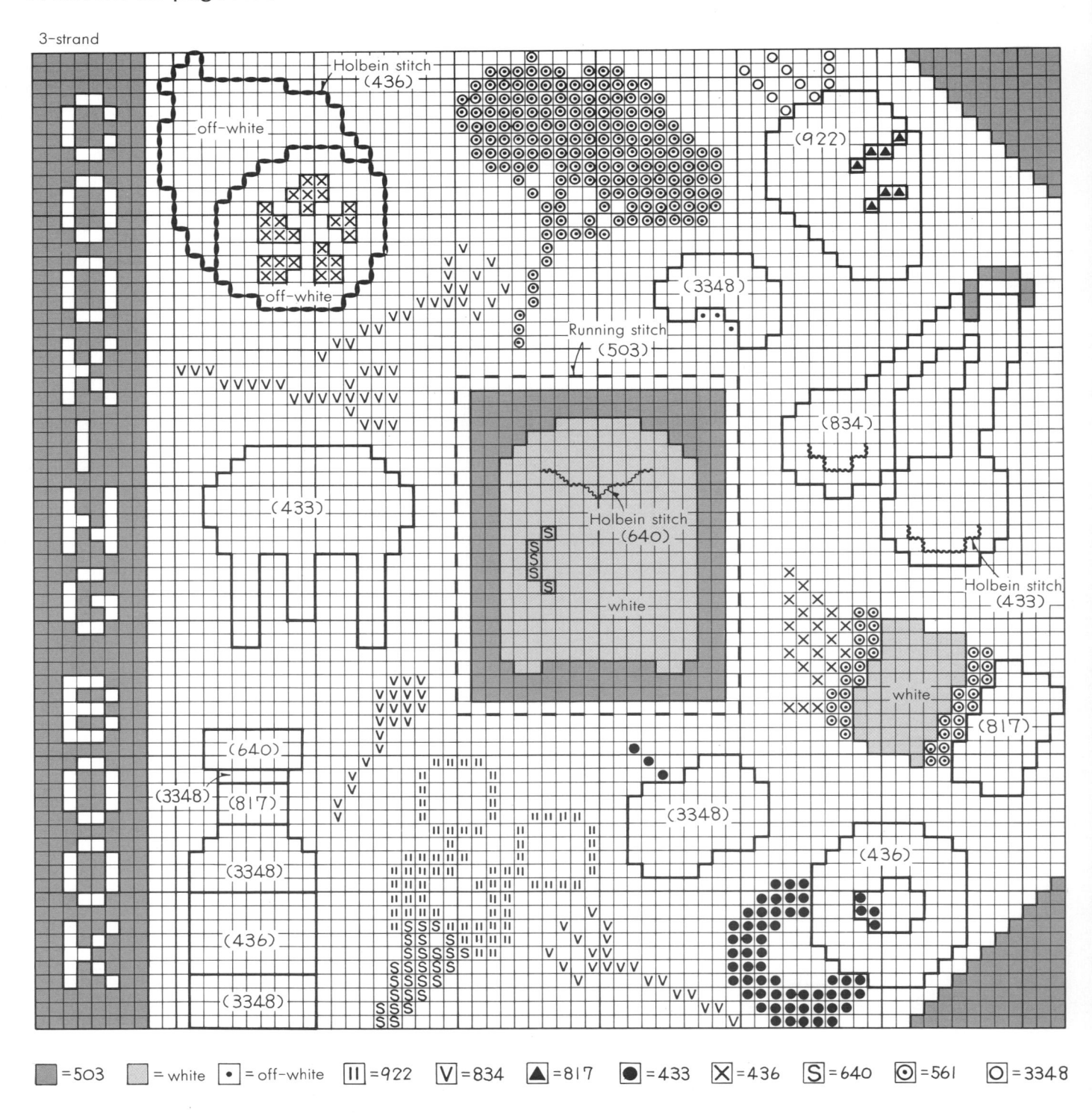

3-strand

■ =503   ▨ = white   • = off-white   ‖ =922   V =834   ▲ =817   ● =433   X =436   S =640   ⊙ =561   O =3348

Lively Kitchen
Parsley, Carrot, Spoons, Candy…
Instructions on page 28. Use Aida cloth.

Savory Warm Stew

Instructions on page 14. Use Aida cloth.

Season with Spice… *Instructions on page 15. Use Aida cloth.*

Welcome to My Kitchen.

Instructions on page 16. Use Aida cloth.

32

I Love Red.

Instructions on page 17. Use Aida cloth.

What is Today's Menu?

Instructions on page 18. Use Aida cloth.

How about Coffee?

Instructions on page 19. Use Aida cloth.

35

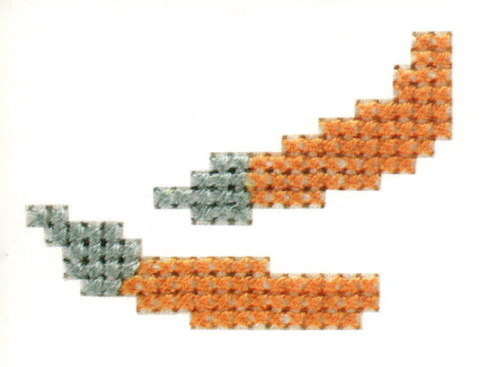

Kitchen Pockets

Are you a good cook? It doesn't matter. This embroidered organizer proves you have other talents.
Instructions on page 51.

Shopping Bag, Pouch, Apron
Instructions on pages 55~57.

Happy Days

So many things make a house a home.
Instructions on page 20. Use Indian cloth. (page 38)
Instructions on page 21. Use Indian cloth. (page 39)

SWEET HOME

AMERICA

LIVING ROOM

A Room with Handmade Goods

Instructions on page 22. Use Aida cloth.

40

Congratulations

Instructions on page 23. Use Aida cloth.

Clock, Mini Cushion

Lovely accesories for the room.
Cheerful embroidery marks the hours.
Instructions on page 53. (Clock)
Instructions on page 54. (Mini Cushion)

43

Frame, Sewing Case, Pin Cushion

*Handmade articles make the best presents.
Instructions on pages 55, 58 and 59.*

☆Shown on page 65.

3-strand except for Running stitch with 2-strand

- △ = 839
- ■ = 895
- ▨ = 834
- V = 310
- ● = 666
- O = 793
- ‖ = white
- · = 758
- × = 727

☆Shown on page 70.

3-strand unless otherwise specfied.

△ = 839　■ = 895　▨ = 834　Ⅴ = 310　● = 666　O = 793　‖ = white　X = 727　▲ = 648

Garment Case

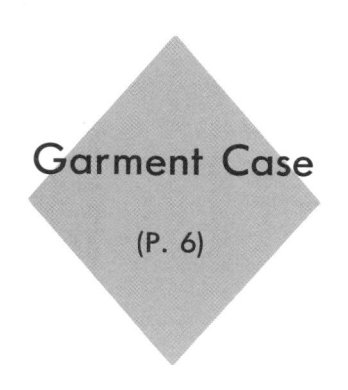

(P. 6)

Materials:
Large-size: 45cm by 99cm(18″×39 5/8″)pink print; 6cm(2 3/8″)square of white Aida cloth; DMC six-strand embroidery floss No. 25: a little each of green(700)and yellow(444): a pair of snaps

Medium-size: 34cm by 93cm(13 5/8″×37 1/4″)pink print; 6cm by 9cm(2 3/8″×3 5/8″) white Aida cloth; DMC six-strand embroidery floss No. 25: a little each of light blue(996)and pink(603); a pair of snaps

Small-size: 26cm by 69cm(10 3/8″×27 5/8″) pink print; 5cm by 6cm(2″×2 3/8″)white Aida cloth; DMC six-strand embroidery floss No. 25: a little each of light blue(996)and pink(603); a pair of snaps

Finished size: Large-size 43cm by 34cm (17 1/4″×13 5/8″), Medium-size 32cm by 31cm (12 3/4″×12 3/8″), Small-size 24cm by 23cm (9 5/8″×9 1/4″)

Instructions(same for all sizes):
1. Sew the embroidered fabric to the front of the print as specified.
2. Turn back both upper and lower seam allowances twice respectively, and stitch.
3. Fold the front and the flap allowance as in the figure with right sides facing. Sew both sides and finish edges with a zigzag sewing machine.

Add the seam allowances shown in parentheses.
Add the 0.5cm(1/4″)seam allowances for embroidery fabric.

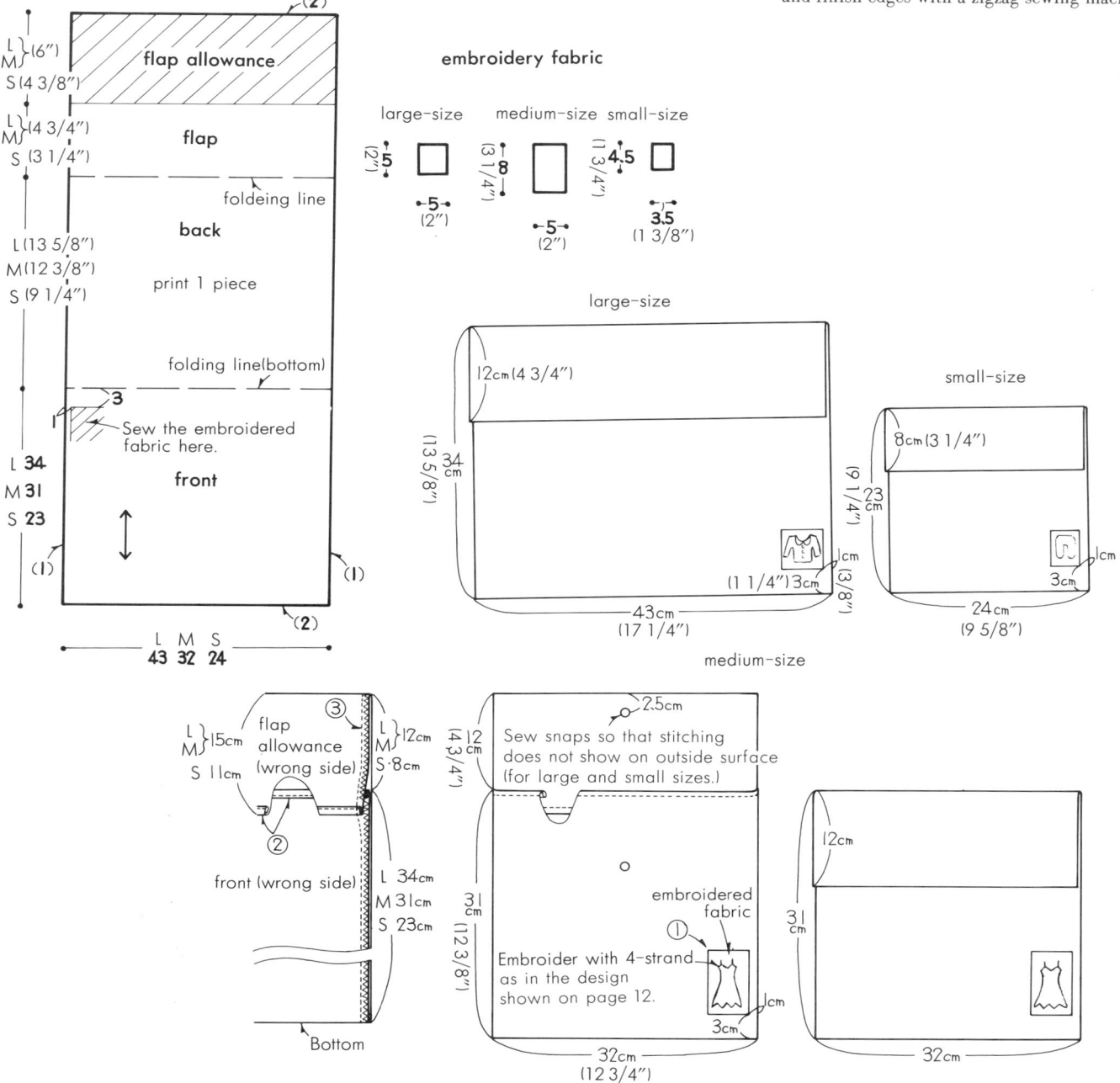

Toiletry Case (P. 6)

Materials:
18cm by 47cm (5 1/4″ × 18 3/4″) pink gingham; 7cm (2 3/4″) square of white Aida cloth; DMC six-strand embroidery floss No. 25: a little each of yellow(444), green(700), light blue(996) and pink(603)
Finished size: 16cm by 12cm (6 3/8″ × 4 3/4″)
Instructions:
Work in the same way as the garment case on page 47 (excepting that the embroidered fabric should be stitched to the flap, not to the front).

Add the seam allowances shown in parentheses.(1.5)

- 12 (4 3/4″) flap allowance
- 1.5 (5/8″)
- 9 (3 5/8″) flap — Sew the embroidered fabric here.
- folding line
- center
- 12 (4 3/4″) back, gingham 1 piece
- (1) (3/8″)
- (1)
- folding line (bottom)
- 11 (4 3/8″) front
- (1.5) (5/8″)
- 16 (6 3/8″)

embroidery fabric
- 6 (2 3/8″)
- 5.5 (2 1/4″)
- seam allowances around edges (0.5) (1/4″)

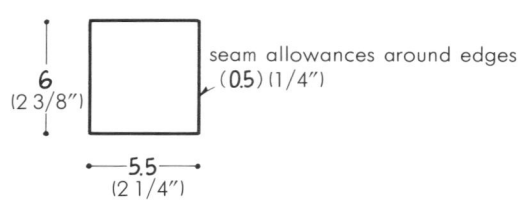

Embroider with 4-strand colors as in the design shown on page 11.

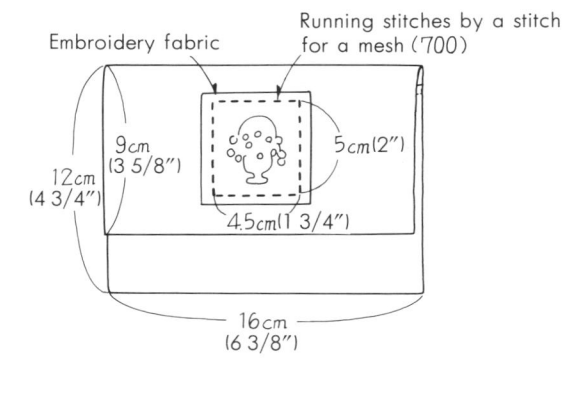

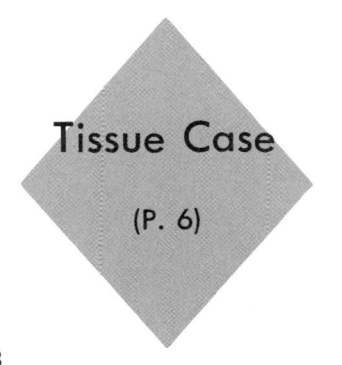

Embroidery fabric / Running stitches by a stitch for a mesh (700)
- 9cm (3 5/8″)
- 12cm (4 3/4″)
- 5cm (2″)
- 4.5cm (1 3/4″)
- 16cm (6 3/8″)

Tissue Case (P. 6)

Materials:
20cm by 15cm (8″ × 6″) white Aida cloth; 20cm by 15cm (8″ × 6″) white cotton; DMC six-strand embroidery floss No. 25: a little each of light blue(996), red(321), green(700), and pink(603)
Finished size: 8.5cm by 12cm (3 3/8″ × 4 3/4″)

Instructions:
1. Match the embroidered outer fabric and the lining, with right sides facing. Sew the slit edges, and turn over.
2. Fold (1) as in the figure with the outer fabric inside, overlapping both slit ends by 0.5cm (1/4″). Sew the upper and lower ends, and finish the edges with a zigzag sewing machine.

Add 1cm seam allowances.
4.5 (1 3/4") — 8.5 (3 3/8") — 4.5
folding line
outer fabric - embroidered fabric
lining - white cotton
1 piece each
center
12 (4 3/4")
17.5 (7")
(3/8") 1

Sew with a zigzag sewing machine. Overlap by 0.5cm (1/4").
embroidered fabric
Sew.
lining (right side)
Ribbon embroidered side

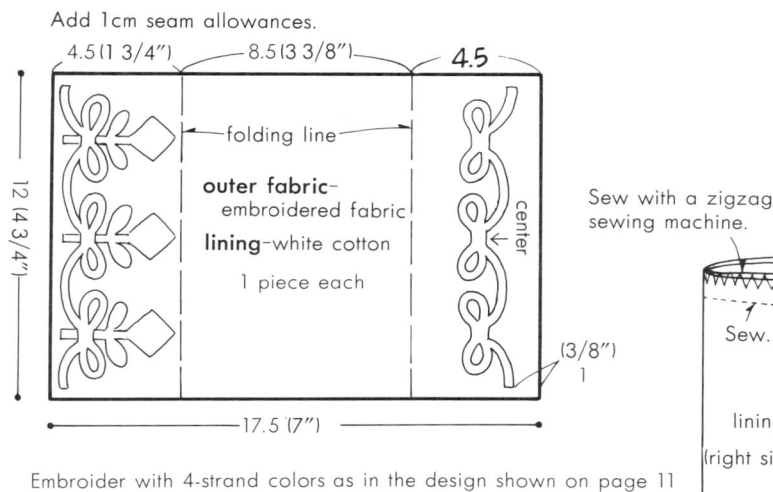

12cm (4 3/4")
8.5cm (3 3/8")

Embroider with 4-strand colors as in the design shown on page 11 (work the joint portions carefully

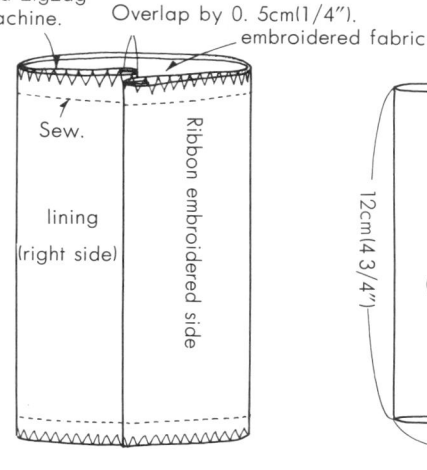

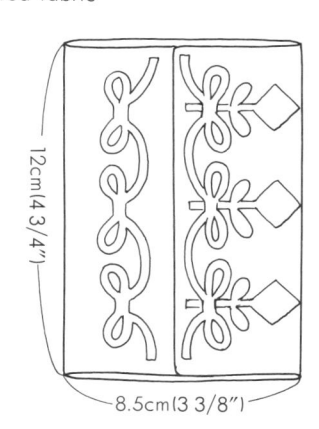

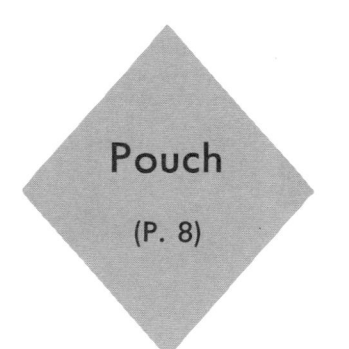

Join with 6 crosses.

Pouch (P. 8)

Materials:
The left: 32cm by 20cm (12 3/4"×8") pink print; a little beige Aide cloth; DMC six-strand embroidery floss No. 25: a little red(321); 1m(40") white rope of 0.3cm(1/8")-diameter
The right: 32cm by 20cm (12 3/4"×8") light blue cotton; a little white Aida cloth; DMC six-strand embroidery floss No. 25: a little each of dark green(890), red(321) and pink(603); 1m(40") light blue rope of 0.3cm(1/8")-diameter
Finished size: 14cm by 16cm (5 5/8"×6 3/8")

Instructions (the same for both):
Sew the embroidered fabric to the front. Match the front and the back, with right sides facing, and sew both sides and the bottom. Turn back the seam allowances of the mouth of the bag twice respectively to make rope casings, and stitch. Pass one rope through around the casings, and another rope the other way around.

4-strand

the left

↑ center

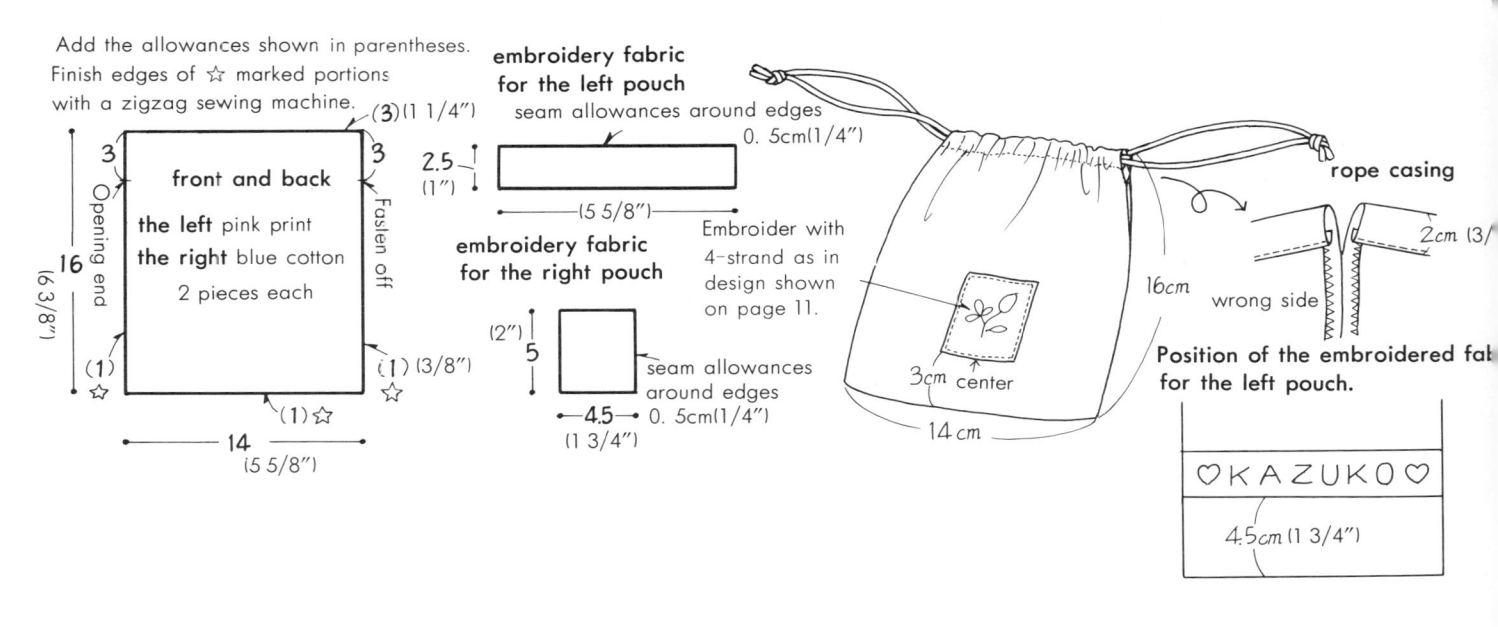

Add the allowances shown in parentheses. Finish edges of ☆ marked portions with a zigzag sewing machine.

embroidery fabric for the left pouch
seam allowances around edges 0.5cm(1/4")
— 5 5/8" —
2.5 (1")

front and back
the left pink print
the right blue cotton
2 pieces each

Opening end 16 (6 3/8")
Fasten off
(1) (3/8")
(1) ☆
14 (5 5/8")
3 (1 1/4")
3

embroidery fabric for the right pouch
Embroider with 4-strand as in design shown on page 11.
(2") 5
4.5 (1 3/4")
seam allowances around edges 0.5cm(1/4")

rope casing
2cm (3/8")
wrong side
16cm
3cm center
14cm

Position of the embroidered fabric for the left pouch.
♡KAZUKO♡
4.5cm (1 3/4")

Mini Sewing Case
(P. 8)

Materials:
25cm by 15cm(10"×6")white Aida cloth; 30cm by 15cm(12"×6")pink print; DMC six-strand embroidery floss No. 25: a little each of dark brown(938), green(700), pink(603), red(321), yellow(444)and light blue(996); 35cm(14")pink satin riboon of 1cm(3/8")-wide; 17cm by 11cm(6 3/4"×4 3/8")quilt foundation; a little synthetic cotton
Finished size: See the figure.

Instructions:
1. Embroider on the outer fabric.
2. Place the outer fabric on the lining with right sides facing. Insert the ribbons and the inner pocket between them(the inner pocket should be placed between the lining and the ribbon), and put the quilt foundation on the outer fabric. Sew along the edges leaving a turning slit. Turn over, and stitch the slit.
3. Make the pin cushion as follows. Fold the embroidered fabric with right side in. Sew the upper and lower ends, and turn over. Fill the synthetic cotton lightly. Stitch the opening.
4. Sew the pin cushion to inside of case with slip stitch.

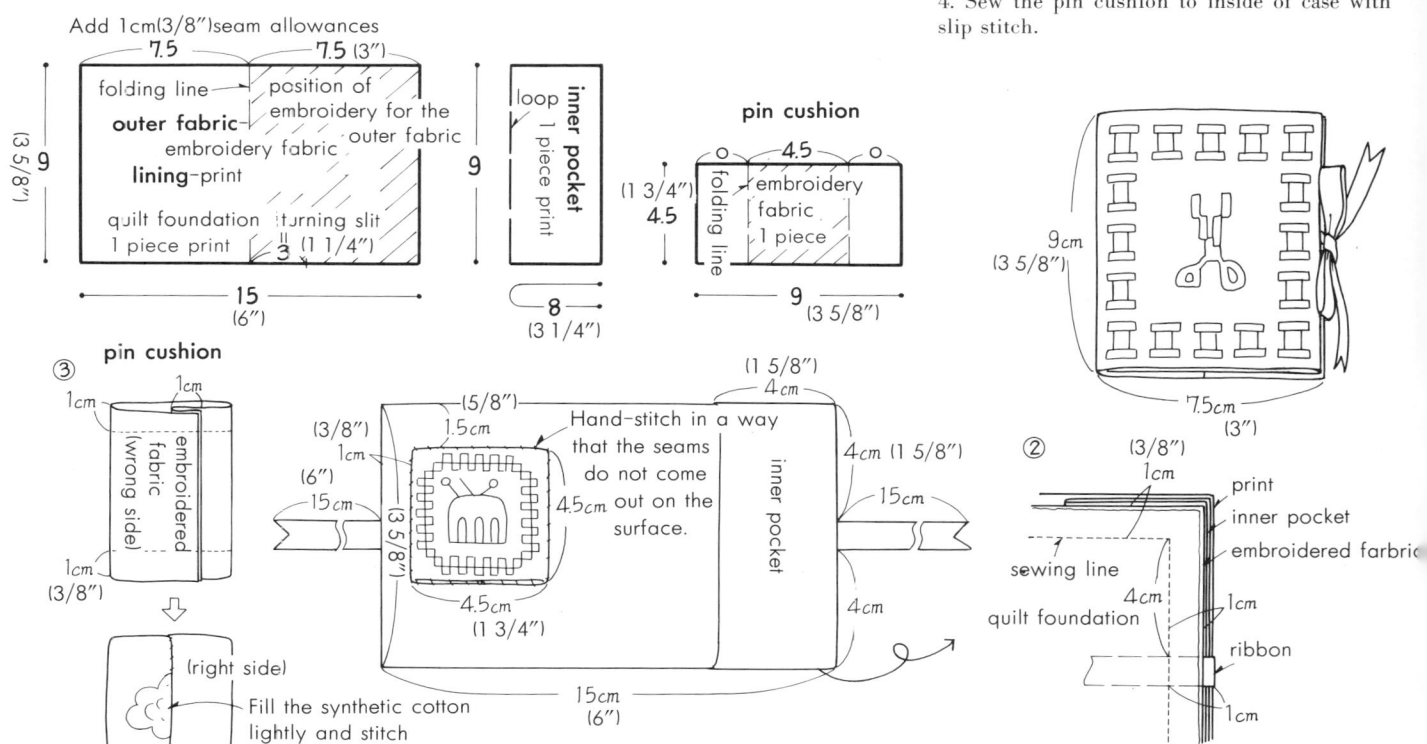

Add 1cm(3/8")seam allowances
7.5 — 7.5 (3")
folding line
position of embroidery for the outer fabric
outer fabric
embroidery fabric
lining-print
quilt foundation turning slit
1 piece print
9 (3 5/8")
3 (1 1/4")
15 (6")

inner pocket
1 piece print
loop
9
8 (3 1/4")

pin cushion
4.5
(1 3/4")
4.5
folding line
embroidery fabric
1 piece
9 (3 5/8")

9cm (3 5/8")
7.5cm (3")

③ **pin cushion**
1cm
1cm
embroidered fabric (wrong side)
1cm (3/8")
(right side)
Fill the synthetic cotton lightly and stitch

(5/8") 1.5cm
(3/8") 1cm
(6") 15cm
4.5cm
4.5cm (1 3/4")
(3 5/8")
Hand-stitch in a way that the seams do not come out on the surface.

(1 5/8") 4cm
inner pocket
4cm (1 5/8")
15cm
4cm
15cm (6")

② (3/8") 1cm
print
inner pocket
embroidered farbric
sewing line
quilt foundation
4cm
1cm
ribbon
1cm

4-strand

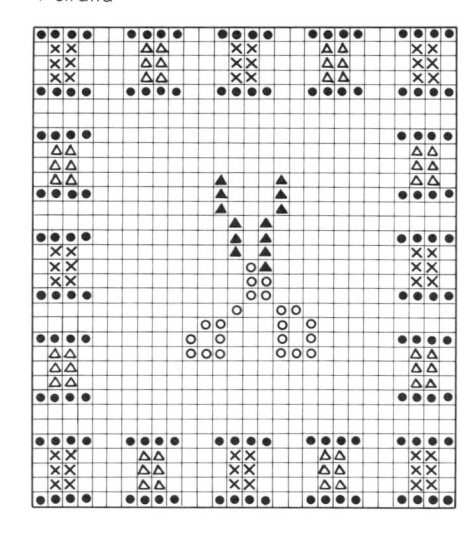

pin cushion
Straight stitch (938)

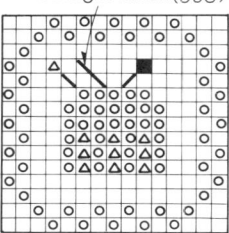

● = 938   △ = 700   × = 603
○ = 321   ▲ = 444   ■ = 996

Kitchen Pocket
(P. 36)

Materials:
50cm by 70cm(20"×28")stripe quilting; 90cm by 40cm(36"×16")natural Aida cloth; DMC six-strand embroidery floss No. 25: a little each of brown(300), reddish brown(355), yellowish brown(435), blue gray(931) and ivory(712); 43cm by 6cm(17 1/4"×2 3/8")iron-on foundation; 2 wood buttons of 2cm(3/4")-diameter; 40cm(16")cotton tape of 0.9cm(3/8")-wide
Finished size: 46cm by 58cm (18 3/8"×23 1/4")

Instructions:
1. Embroider the pocket and the small bag. Finish the upper edges of the pockets as in the figure.
2. Turn back allowance of both sides of the base fabric, and sew. Make a pole casing, and sew the lower end. Sew the pockets to the base fabric. Stitch partitions of each pocket, and put buttons.
3. Sew small bags in the order of (a), (b) and (c). Pass a cotton tape through the casing. Hang the bags at the buttons.

Add 1cm(3/8")seam allowances unless specified in parentheses.
Finish ☆ marked edges with a zigzag sewing machine.

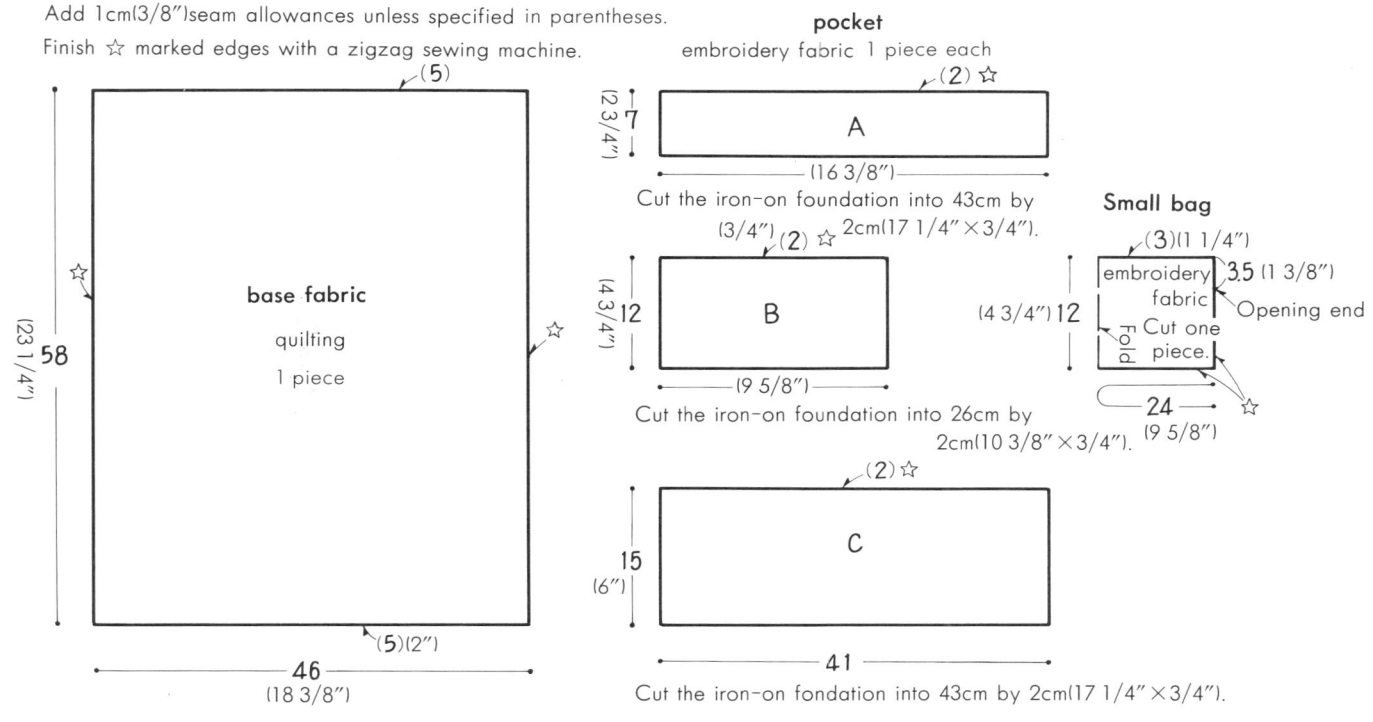

base fabric
quilting
1 piece
58 (23 1/4")
46 (18 3/8")
(5)(2")

pocket
embroidery fabric 1 piece each

A 7 (2 3/4") (16 3/8")
Cut the iron-on foundation into 43cm by 2cm(17 1/4"×3/4").

B 12 (4 3/4") (9 5/8")
Cut the iron-on foundation into 26cm by 2cm(10 3/8"×3/4").

C 15 (6") 41
Cut the iron-on fondation into 43cm by 2cm(17 1/4"×3/4").

Small bag
embroidery fabric
(3)(1 1/4") 3.5 (1 3/8") Opening end
Fold Cut one piece.
24 (9 5/8")

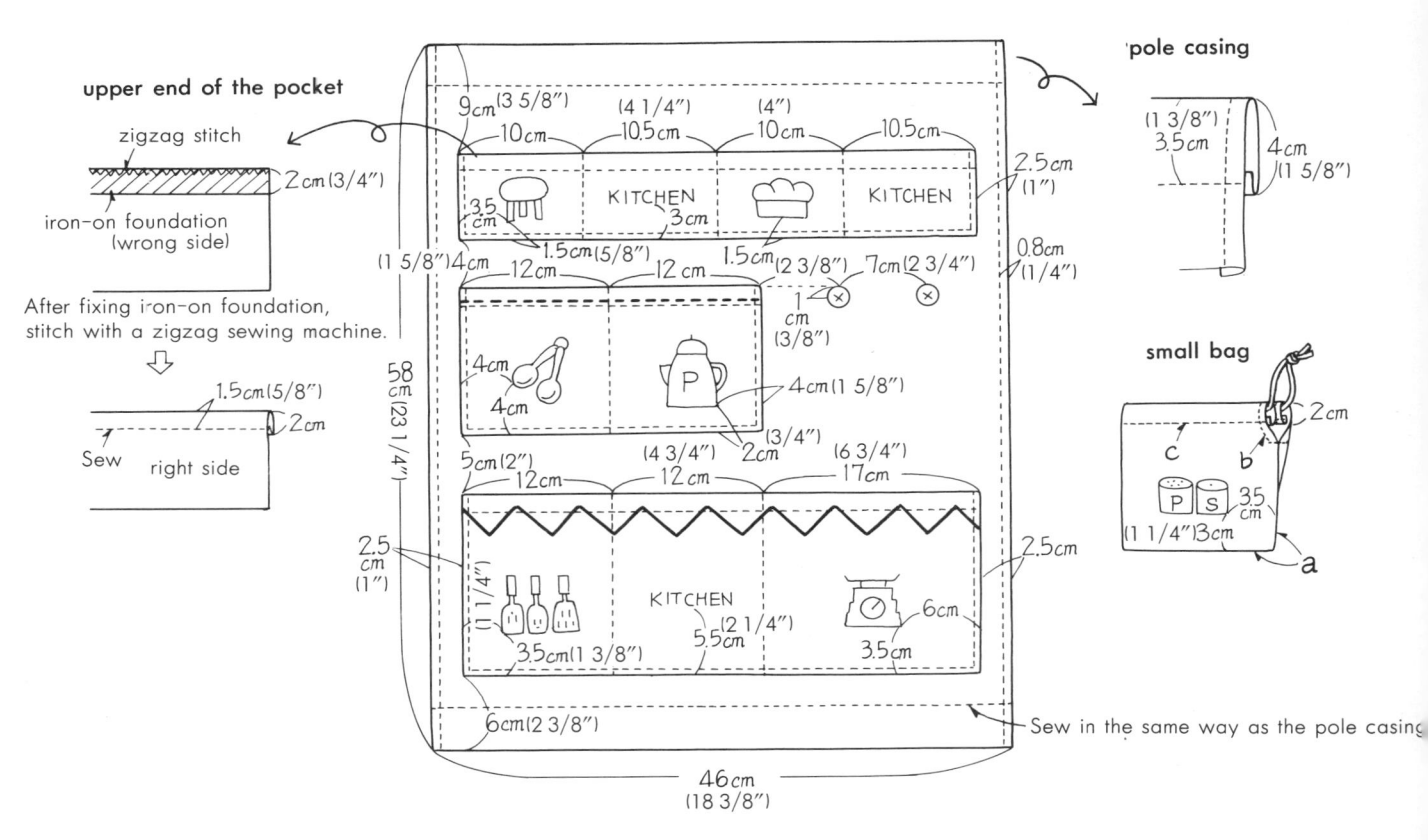

upper end of the pocket

zigzag stitch

iron-on foundation (wrong side)

2 cm (3/4")

After fixing iron-on foundation, stitch with a zigzag sewing machine.

1.5 cm (5/8")
2 cm
Sew — right side

pole casing

(1 3/8") 3.5 cm — 4 cm (1 5/8")

small bag

c b
P S 3.5 cm
(1 1/4") 3 cm
a

Sew in the same way as the pole casing

= 300
● = 355
○ = 435
✕ = 931
= 712

Holbein stitch (712)
Holbein stitch (712)
Holbein stitch (435)
Holbein stitch (355)

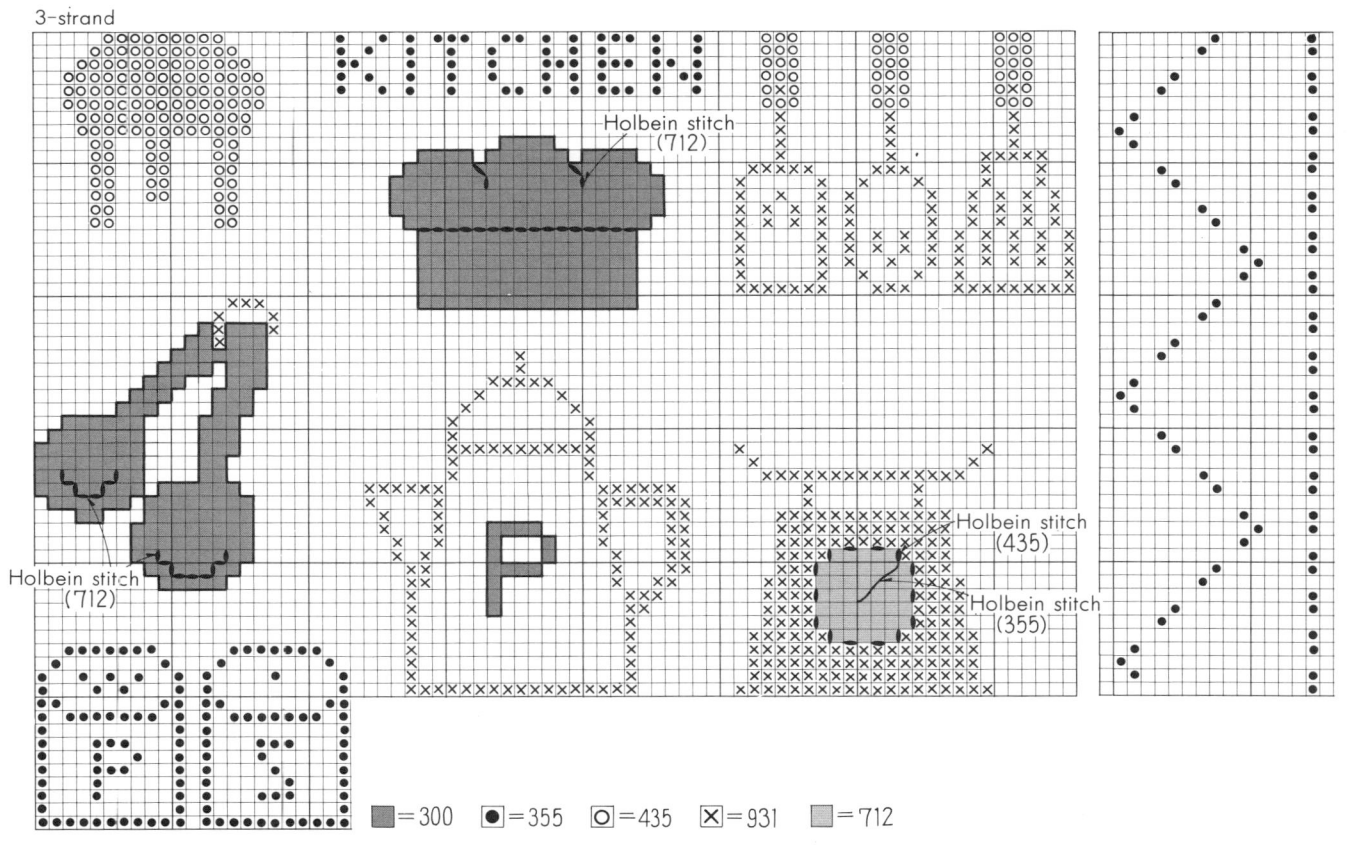

3-strand

52

Clock

(P. 42)

Materials:
25cm(10")square of natural Aida cloth; DMC six-strand embroidery floss No. 25: a little each of grayish green(502), somber pink(223), Oxford blue(336), brown(400), brilliant brown(782), beige(422), deep red(347), olive green(3346), red(817) and black(310); a frame of 23cm(9 1/4")-outside diameter and 19cm(7 5/8")-inside diameter; a set of commercially sold clock parts; glue

Finished size: the same as the frame size

Instructions:
After matching the centers of the embroidery fabric and the pattern, work the design, counting meshes from the center. Cut the fabric into a circle of 25cm(10")-diameter, and stitch along edge with long stitches. Make a hole at the center of the fabric. Apply glue to the clockface. Cover the clockface with the cloth and pull the stitches at the back to secure. Assemble the clock, and put in the frame.

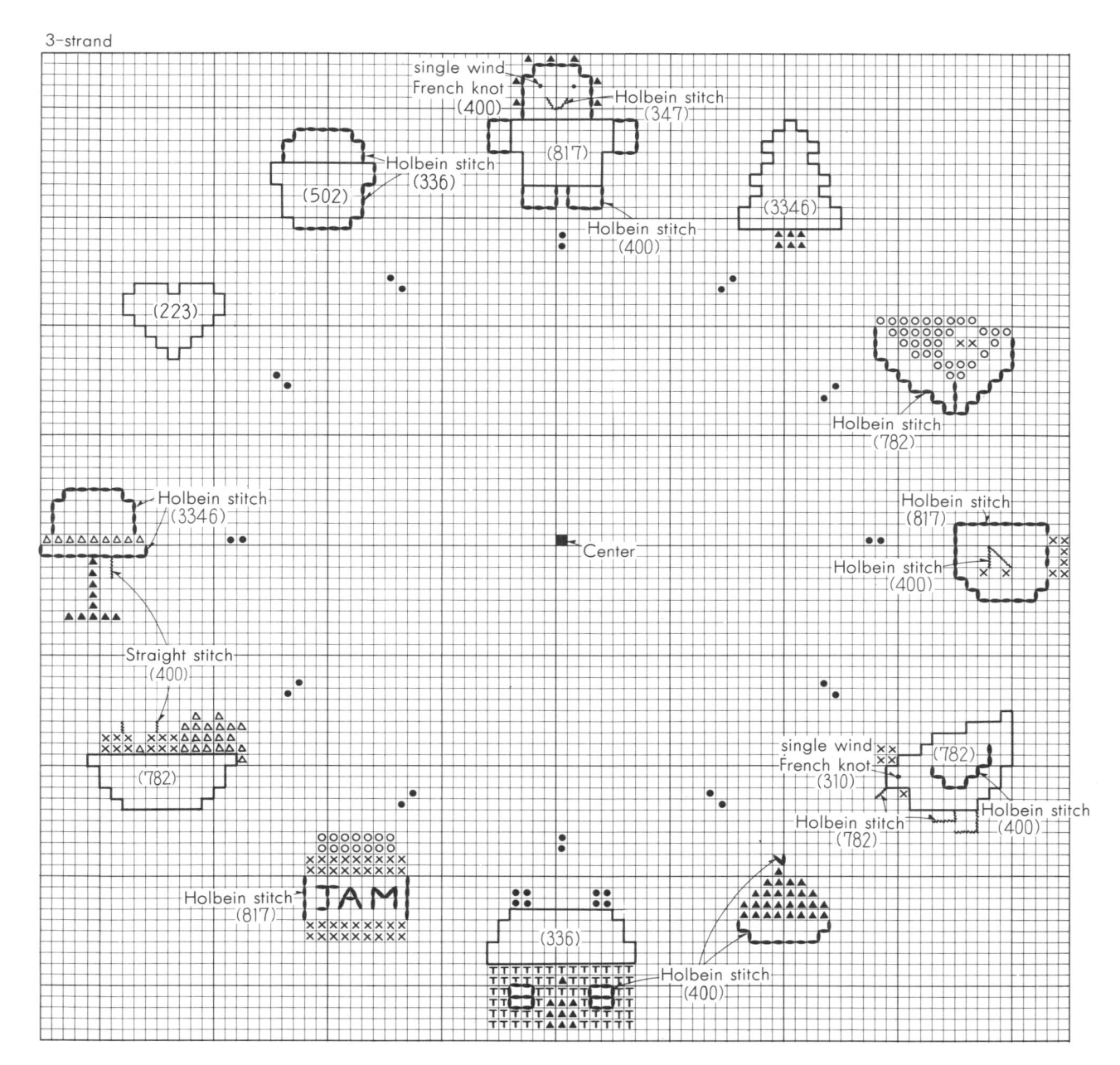

▲=400 O=782 T=422 ●=347 △=3346 ✕=817

Mini Cushion

(P. 43)

Materials:

The left: 74cm by 34cm(29 5/8″×13 5/8″)grayish brown check; 14cm by 13cm(5 5/8″×5 1/4″)natural Aida cloth; DMC six-strand embroidery floss No. 25: a little each of brown(801), light brown(422), reddish brown(300,400), olive green(470), red(347), gray(647) and grayish green(502); a 28cm(11 1/4″)zipper; a 30cm(12″)square inner bag containing polyester fiberfill

The middle: 74cm by 34cm(29 5/8″×13 5/8″) grayish brown check; 12cm(4 3/4″)square natural Aida Cloth; DMC six-strand embroidery floss No.25: a little each of brown(801, 433), light brown(422), grayish brown(3032), deep red(221) and gray(646); a 28cm(11 1/4″)zipper; a 30cm (12″)square inner bag containing polyester fiberfill

The right: 74cm by 34cm(29 5/8″×13 5/8″) olive green check; 17cm(6 3/4″)square grayish green cotton; 12cm(4 3/4″)square natural Aida cloth; DMC six-strand embroidery floss No.25: a little each of brown(433, 632), dark brown(898), grayish brown(640), yellowish brown(436), gray(647), olive green(470), red(347), grayish green(502), reddish brown(918) and black(310); a 28cm(11 1/4″)zipper; a 30cm(12″)square inner bag containing polyester fiberfill

Finished size: 32cm(12 3/4″)square

Instructions(same for the three):
Sew the embroidered fabric to the front as shown in the figure. Sew up the back pieces with a zipper applied. Sew the front and the back together, with right sides facing.

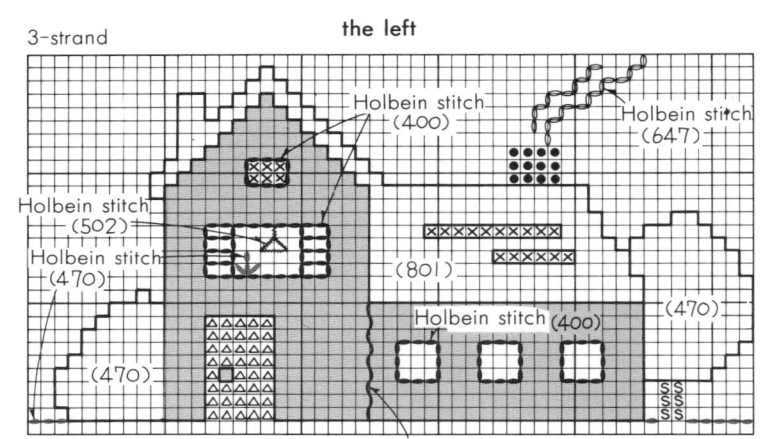

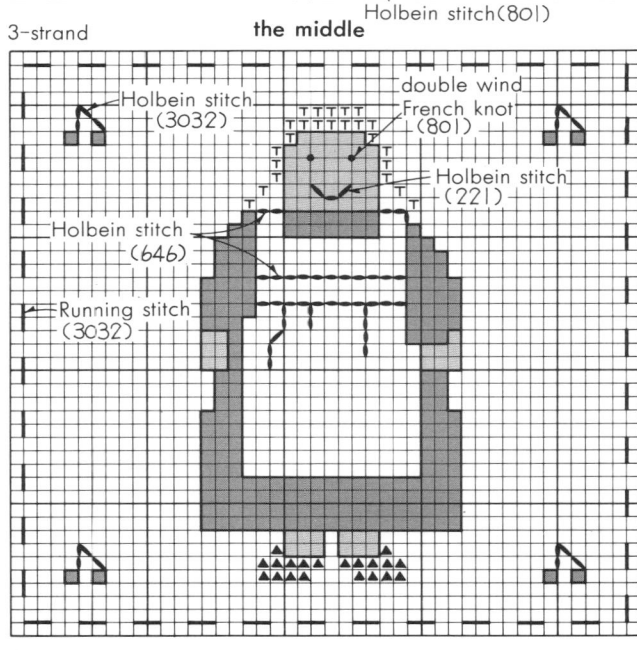

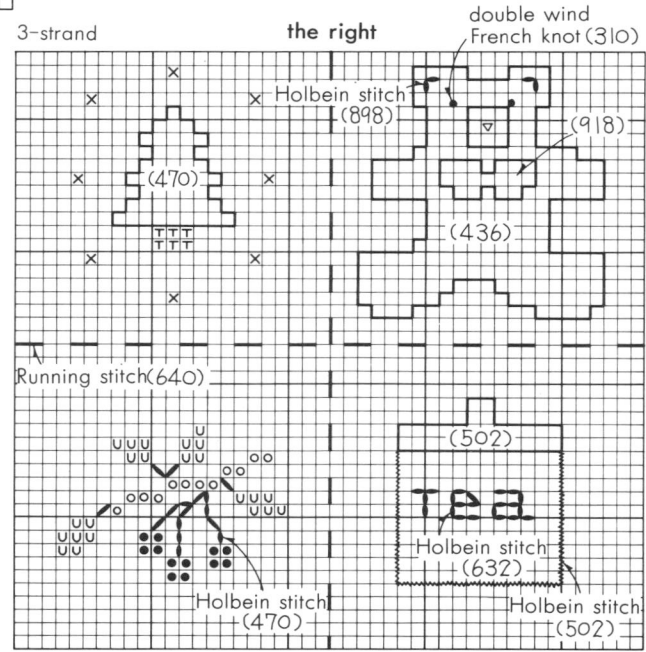

Add 1cm(3/8")seam allowances unless specified in parentheses.

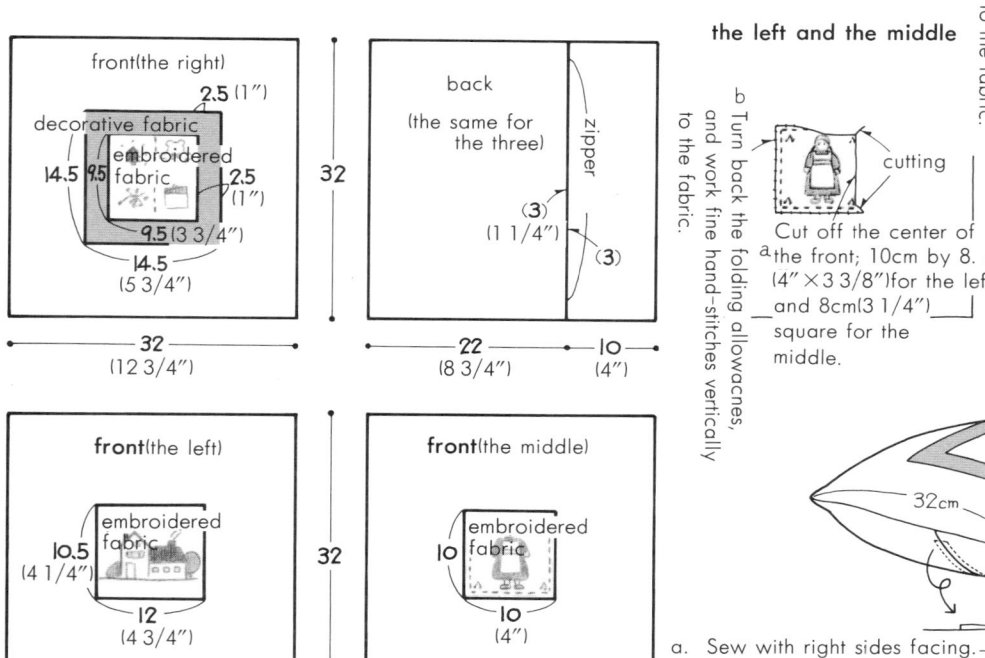

How to apply the embroidered fabrics

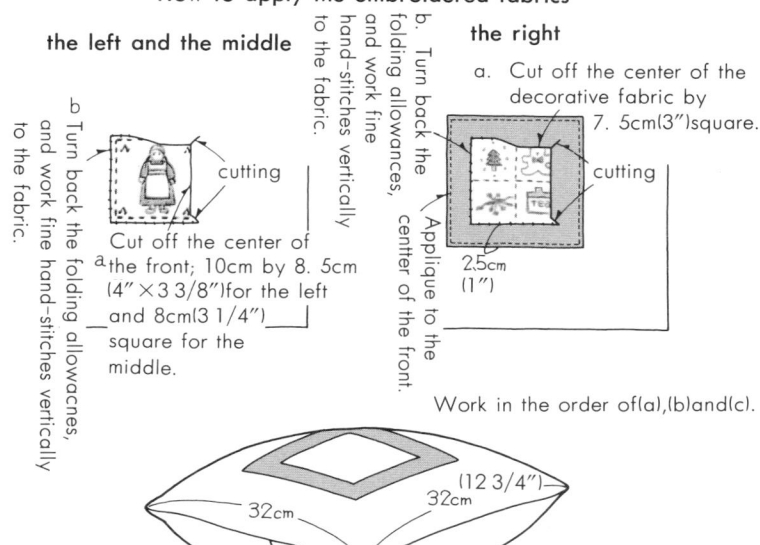

the left and the middle

the right

front(the right) 2.5 (1")
decorative fabric
14.5 9.5 embroidered fabric 2.5 (1")
9.5 (3 3/4")
14.5 (5 3/4")
32
32 (12 3/4")

back (the same for the three)
zipper
(3)
(3) (1 1/4")
22 (8 3/4") 10 (4")

b. Turn back the folding allowacnes, and work fine hand-stitches vertically to the fabric.

Cut off the center of the front; 10cm by 8.5cm (4"×3 3/8")for the left and 8cm(3 1/4") square for the middle.

a. Cut off the center of the decorative fabric by 7.5cm(3")square.

b. Turn back the folding allowances, and work fine hand-stitches vertically to the fabric.

cutting

2.5cm (1")
Applique to the center of the front.

Work in the order of(a),(b)and(c).

front(the left)
embroidered fabric
10.5 (4 1/4")
12 (4 3/4")
32
32 (12 3/4")

front(the middle)
embroidered fabric
10 (4")
10 (4")
32
32

32cm (12 3/4")
32cm

Sew(a)first.
a. Sew with right sides facing.
3cm (1 1/4")
b. Turn over, and sew a zipper.

Frame (P. 44)

Materials:
35cm by 30cm(14"×12")white Aida cloth; DMC six-strand embroidery floss No. 25: 1.5 skeins of red(666); a frame of 24cm by 19cm(9 5/8"×7 5/8")-inner size

Finished size: See the inner size of the frame(see the photo on page 41 for the size of the embroidery).

Instructions:
Embroider as the chart on 23 page using 3-strand red floss, and put in a frame.

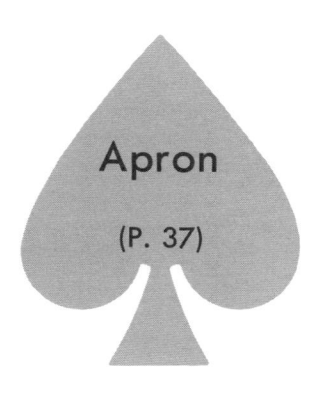

Apron (P. 37)

Materials:
90cm by 220cm(36"×88")light beige washer-processed(wrinke processed)sheeting; 20cm by 11cm(8"×4 3/8")dark beige Aida cloth; DMC six-strand embroidery floss No. 25: a little each of reddish brown(355), yellowish brown(435) and grayish brown(640)

Finished size: 102cm(40 3/4")in length

Instructions:
1. Sew the embroidered pieces to the pockets, and finish the top edges. Sew the pockets to the front body.
2. Sew the shoulders together, with right sides facing. Finish the edges together, with a zigzag sewing machine.
3. Turn the seam allowacnes of shoulders toward the back body. Bind the armholes with bias tape.
4. Sew the sides together, with right sides facing. Finish the edges together with a zigzag sewing machine. Turn the seam allowances toward the back body, and fasten it at the armholes.
5. Make straps. After binding the neckline with a bias tape, finish back centers continuously, with the straps inserted. Fasten the straps at the edges to reinforce.
6. Finish the hem.

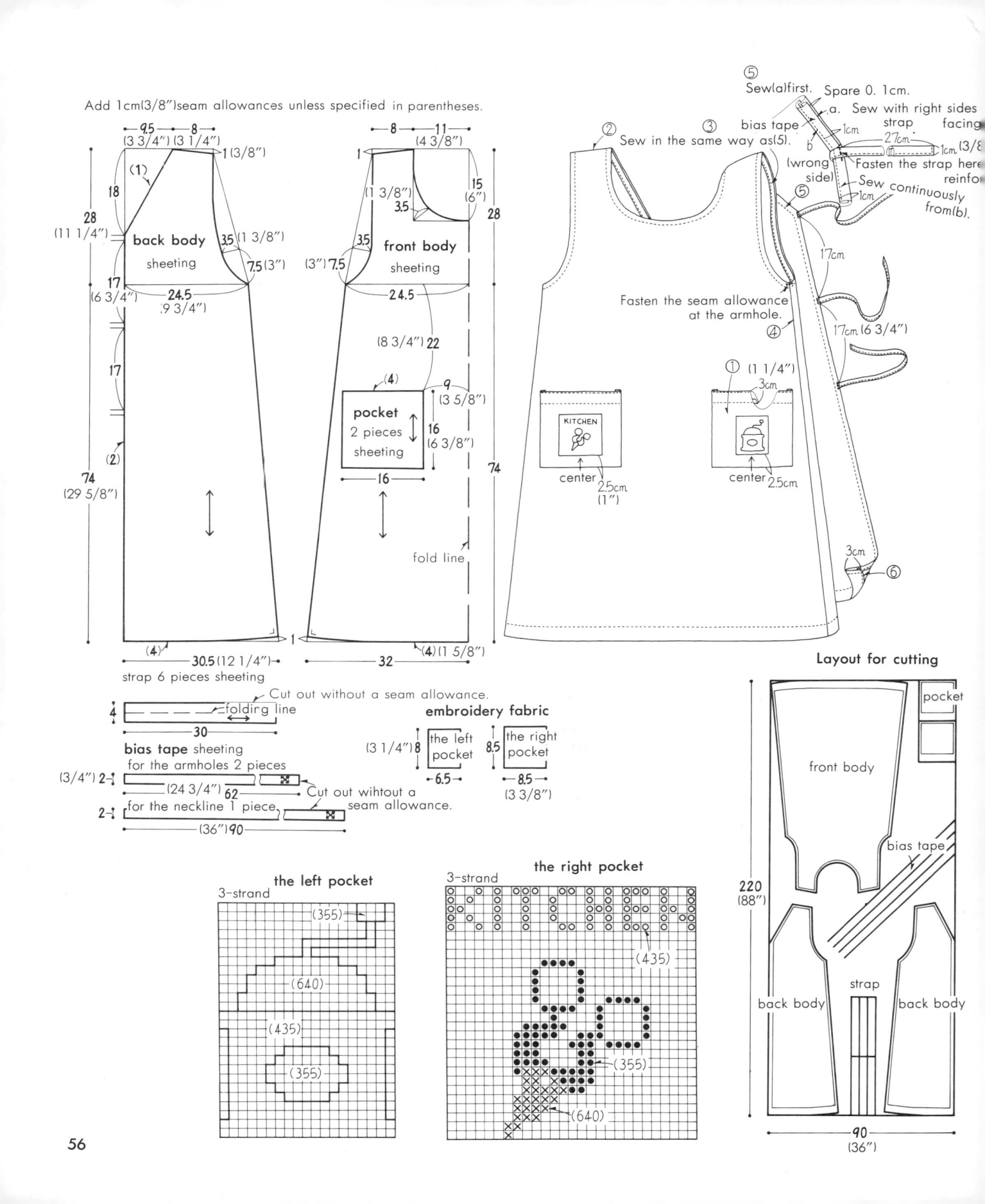

Add 1cm(3/8") seam allowances unless specified in parentheses.

back body sheeting
- 9.5 (3 3/4") — 8 (3 1/4")
- 1 (3/8")
- 18
- (1)
- 28 (11 1/4")
- 3.5 (1 3/8")
- 7.5 (3")
- 17 (6 3/4")
- 24.5 (9 3/4")
- 17
- (2)
- 74 (29 5/8")
- (4)
- 30.5 (12 1/4")
- 1

front body sheeting
- 8 — 11 (4 3/8")
- 1
- 15 (6")
- 3.5 (1 3/8")
- 28
- 3.5 (3") 7.5
- 24.5
- (8 3/4") 22
- (4)
- 9 (3 5/8")
- **pocket 2 pieces sheeting**
- 16 (6 3/8")
- 16
- 74
- fold line
- (4) (1 5/8")
- 32

strap 6 pieces sheeting
- 4
- Cut out without a seam allowance.
- folding line
- 30

bias tape sheeting
- (3/4") 2 1/2 — for the armholes 2 pieces — (24 3/4") 62
- 2 1/2 — for the neckline 1 piece — (36") 90
- Cut out without a seam allowance.

embroidery fabric
- the left pocket: (3 1/4") 8 × 6.5
- the right pocket: 8.5 × 8.5 (3 3/8")

Assembly diagram
- ② Sew in the same way as ⑤.
- ⑤ Sew (a) first. Spare 0.1cm.
- a. Sew with right sides facing
- bias tape, strap
- 27cm, 1cm (3/8")
- b (wrong side)
- Fasten the strap here, reinforce
- Sew continuously from (b).
- 1cm
- 17cm
- ③
- ④ Fasten the seam allowance at the armhole.
- 17cm (6 3/4")
- ① (1 1/4") 3cm
- KITCHEN
- center 2.5cm (1")
- center 2.5cm
- 3cm
- ⑥

the left pocket
3-strand
- (355)
- (640)
- (435)
- (355)

the right pocket
3-strand
- (435)
- (355)
- (640)

Layout for cutting
- pocket
- front body
- bias tape
- 220 (88")
- back body — strap — back body
- 90 (36")

Shopping Bag
(P. 37)

Materials:
90cm by 80cm (36"×32") wrinkle processed dark brown sheeting; 40cm (16") square dark brown check; 90cm by 10cm (36"×4") print; 90cm by 10cm (36"×4") natural Aida cloth; DMC six-strand embroidery floss No.25 : a little each of dark green (500), beige (842) and grayish brown (640); 90cm by 40cm (36"×16") interfacing; 90cm (36") cotton tape of 2.5cm (1")-wide
Finished size: See the figure

Instructions:
1. Make 2 pieces each of (b) and (e), sewing the embroidered pieces to the print pieces as in the figure.
2. Join (a) through (f) as shown in the figure to make the front and the back.
3. Make 2 pairs of the top pieces matched with right sides facing. Sew one side of each pair, with the cotton tapes inserted.
4. Open (3). Sew them together with right sides facing.
5. Match the front and the back with right sides facing, with the top pieces turned up as in the figure. Sew both sides and the bottom. Finish the edges with a zigzag sewing machine.
6. Make straps. Fold the top to the inside, and turn back the seam allowance. Insert the straps. Hand-stitch along the seams on the lining.

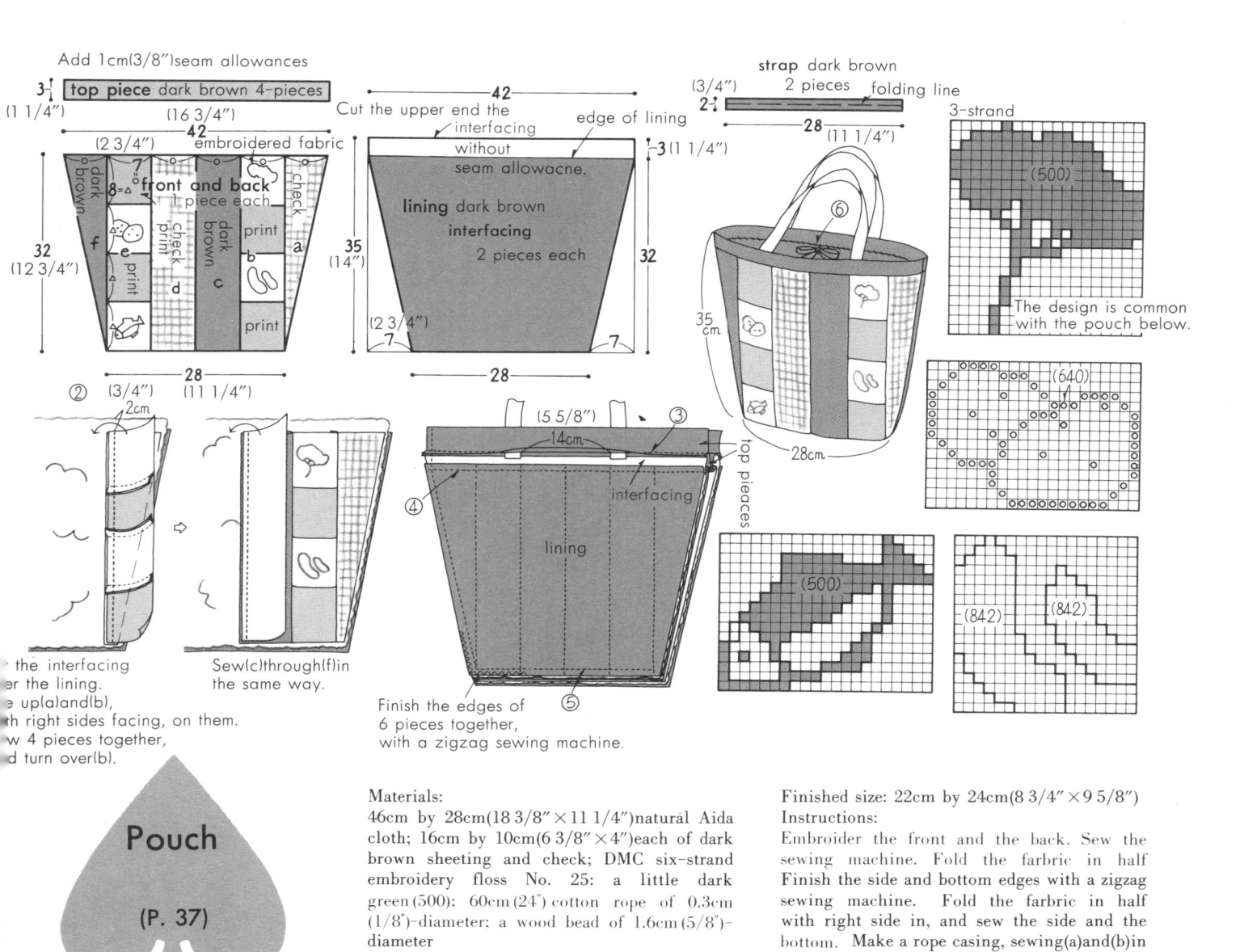

Add 1cm (3/8") seam allowances

Pouch
(P. 37)

Materials:
46cm by 28cm (18 3/8"×11 1/4") natural Aida cloth; 16cm by 10cm (6 3/8"×4") each of dark brown sheeting and check; DMC six-strand embroidery floss No. 25: a little dark green (500); 60cm (24") cotton rope of 0.3cm (1/8")-diameter; a wood bead of 1.6cm (5/8")-diameter

Finished size: 22cm by 24cm (8 3/4"×9 5/8")

Instructions:
Embroider the front and the back. Sew the sewing machine. Fold the fabric in half. Finish the side and bottom edges with a zigzag sewing machine. Fold the fabric in half with right side in, and sew the side and the bottom. Make a rope casing, sewing (a) and (b) in order. After passing the rope through the casing, then a wood bead, tie a knot.

57

Add 1cm(3/8") seam allowances unless specified in parentheses.

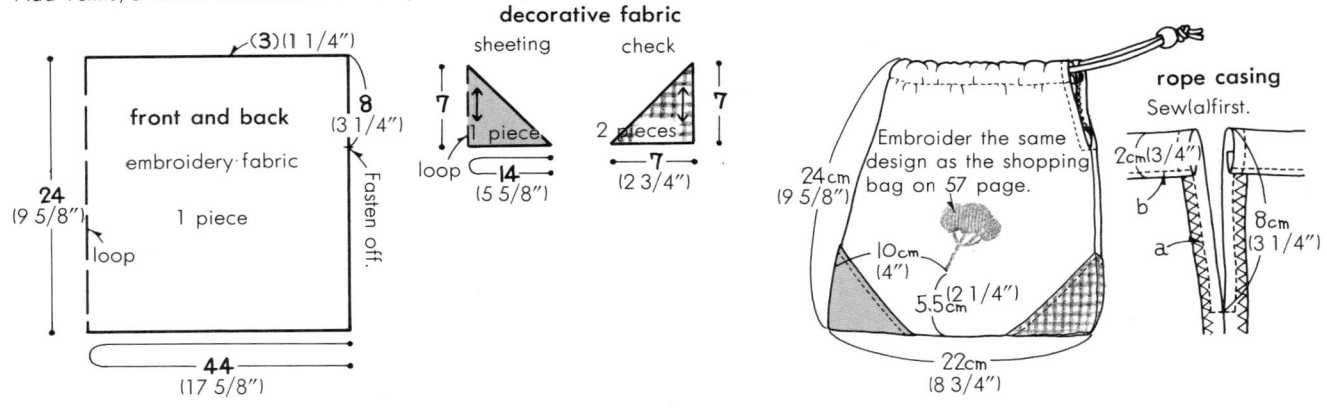

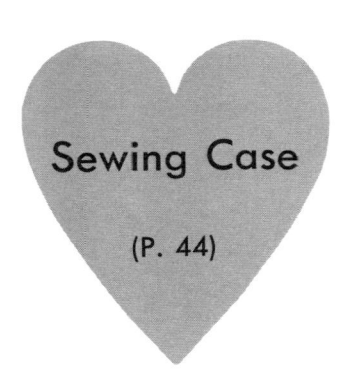

front and back
embroidery fabric
1 piece
24 (9 5/8")
44 (17 5/8")
(3)(1 1/4")
8 (3 1/4")
loop
Fasten off.

decorative fabric
sheeting — 1 piece — loop
14 (5 5/8")
7
check — 2 pieces
7
(2 3/4")

Embroider the same design as the shopping bag on 57 page.
24cm (9 5/8")
22cm (8 3/4")
10cm (4")
5.5 (2 1/4")

rope casing
Sew (a) first.
2cm (3/4")
8cm (3 1/4")
a
b

Sewing Case (P. 44)

Materials:
34cm by 51cm (13 5/8" × 20 3/8") moss green check; 12cm by 10cm (4 3/4" × 4") white Aida cloth; DMC six-strand embroidery floss No. 25: a little each of olive green(986), emerald green(911,912), grayish green(368), brown(632), somber yellow(677), charcoal gray(413), gray(452) and red(666); 2 buttons of 1.5cm (5/8")-diameter

Finished size: 15cm by 17.5cm (6" × 7")
Instructions:
1. Sew the embroidered fabric to the outer flap.
2. Match the outer fabric and the lining with right sides facing. Sew them together along the opening edge, leaving a turning slit.
3. Fold (2) as in the figure. Sew both sides and the upper end, leaving the bottom, and turn over.
4. Sew up the turning slit. Make the buttonholes and stitch. Add buttons.

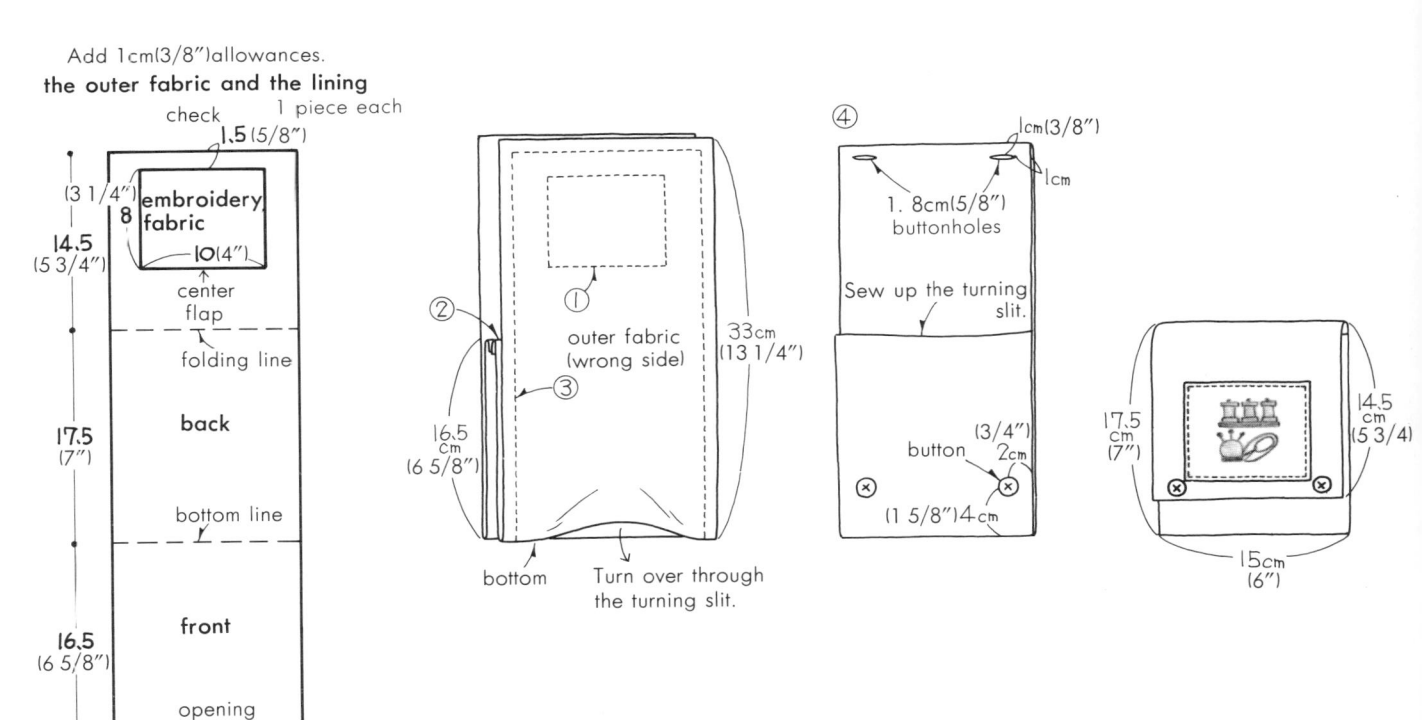

Add 1cm(3/8") allowances.
the outer fabric and the lining
check — 1 piece each
1.5 (5/8")
embroidery fabric
8
10 (4")
14.5 (5 3/4")
(3 1/4")
center flap
folding line
back
17.5 (7")
bottom line
front
16.5 (6 5/8")
opening
turning slit
15 (6")

② ① ③
outer fabric (wrong side)
33cm (13 1/4")
16.5 cm (6 5/8")
bottom
Turn over through the turning slit.

④
1cm(3/8")
1cm
1.8cm(5/8") buttonholes
Sew up the turning slit.
button
2cm (3/4")
4cm (1 5/8")

17.5 cm (7")
14.5 cm (5 3/4")
15cm (6")

3-strand unless otherwise specified.

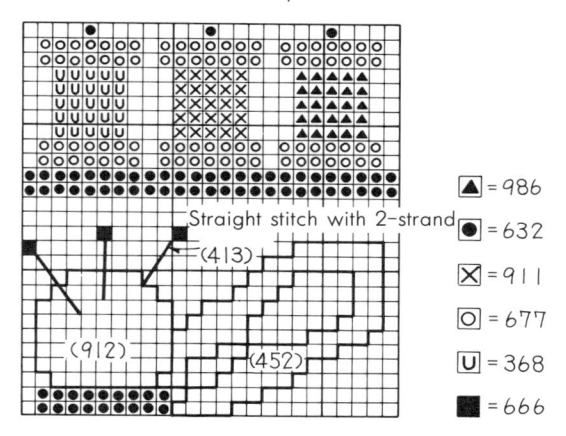

▲ = 986
● = 632
✗ = 911
○ = 677
U = 368
■ = 666

Straight stitch with 2-strand
(413)
(912)
(452)

Pin Cushion
(P. 44)

Materials:
Top cushion: 23cm by 12cm(9 1/4"×4 3/4") white Aida cloth; DMC six-strand embroidery floss No. 25: a little each of red(666) and pink(605); a little synthetic cotton
Middle cushion: 10cm(4")square red check; 10cm(4")square white(1)Aida Cloth; DMC six-strand embroidery floss No. 25: a little red(666); a little synthetic cotton

Lower cushion: 20cm by 10cm(8"×4")moss green check; 10cm by 6cm(4"×2 3/8")white Aida cloth; DMC six-strand embroidery floss No. 25: a little each of green(700)and brown(632); a little synthetic cotton
Finished size: See the figure.
Instructions(same for all three):
1. Embroider the front. (In making the lower cushion, join the embroidered fabric and the check together to make the front.)
2. Sew the front and the back together, leaving a turning slit, with right sides facing. Turn over. Fill with synthetic cotton, and stitch the turning slit. For the top cushion, apply a tassel at a corner.

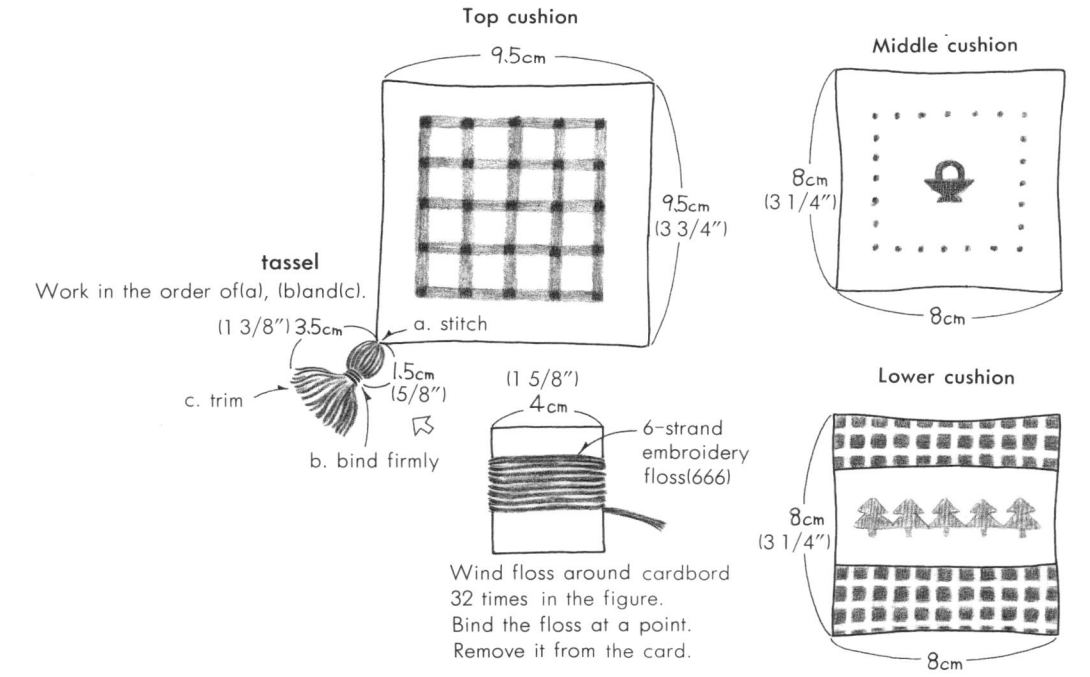

Top cushion
9.5cm
9.5cm (3 3/4")

tassel
Work in the order of(a), (b)and(c).
(1 3/8") 3.5cm
a. stitch
c. trim
1.5cm (5/8")
b. bind firmly

(1 5/8")
4cm
6-strand embroidery floss(666)
Wind floss around cardbord 32 times in the figure. Bind the floss at a point. Remove it from the card.

Middle cushion
8cm (3 1/4")
8cm

Lower cushion
8cm (3 1/4")
8cm

The chart is on the following page.

Top cushion

Add 1cm(3/8")seam allowacnes.

front and back 1 piece each
embroidery fabric
Embroider the front only.

9.5 (3 3/4")
9.5

turning slit

■ = 666   ▦ = 605   ● = 632   ○ = 700

Middle cushion

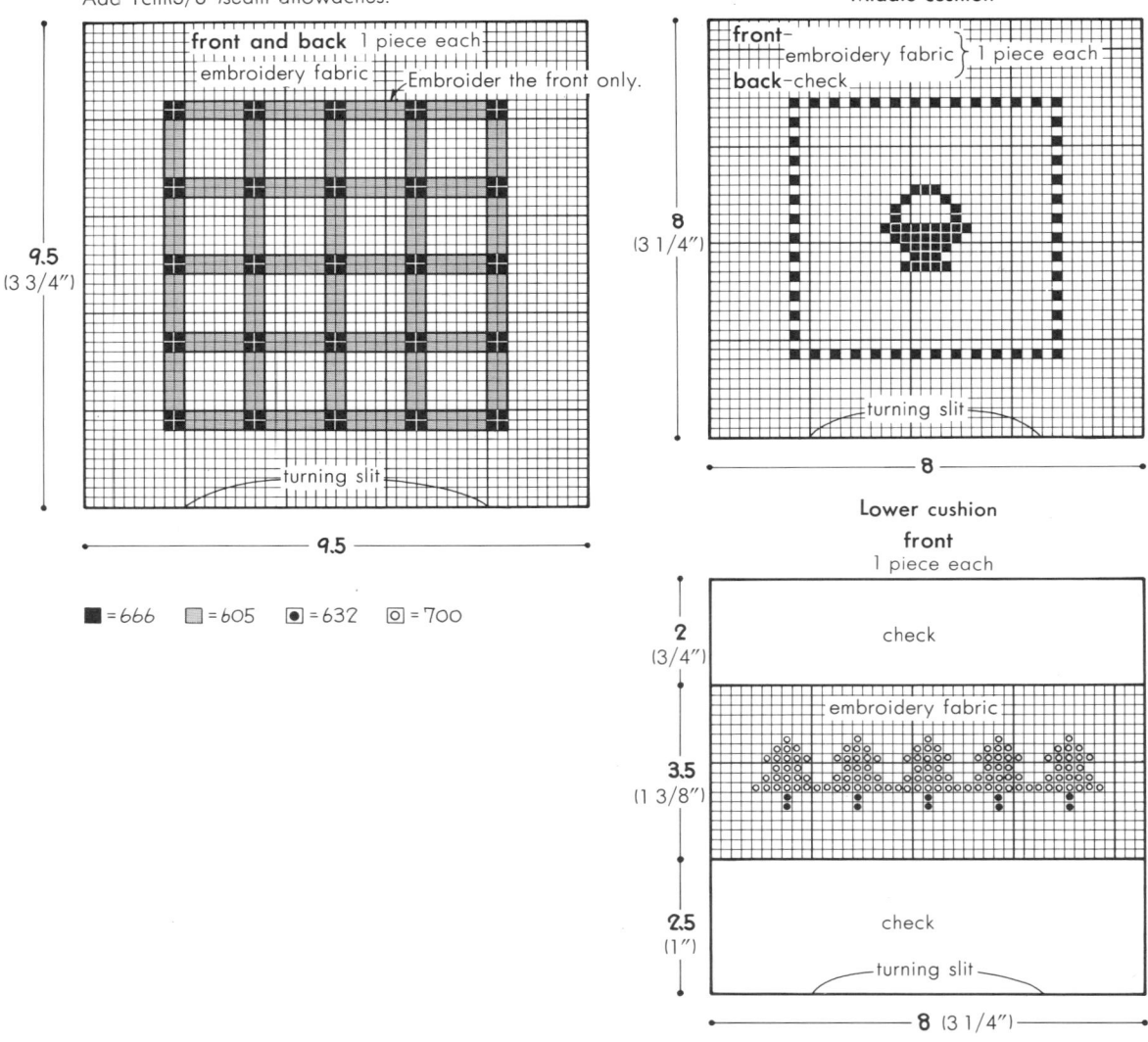

front- embroidery fabric } 1 piece each
back- check

8 (3 1/4")
8

turning slit

Lower cushion

front
1 piece each

2 (3/4") check

3.5 (1 3/8") embroidery fabric

2.5 (1") check

turning slit

8 (3 1/4")

Cut check into 10cm(4")square for the back.

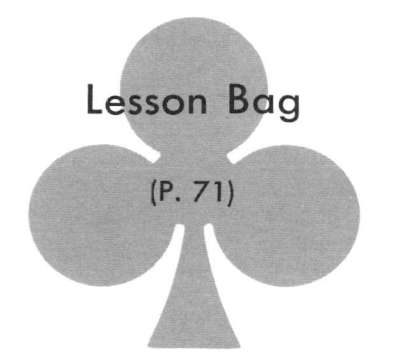

Lesson Bag (P. 71)

Materials:
The left bag: 90cm by 35cm(36"×14")green check quilting; 90cm by 10cm(36"×4")green check cotton; 40cm by 10cm(16"×4")white Aida cloth; DMC six-strand embroidery floss No. 25; a little each of cream(745), brown(300), light brown(950), green(561), red(817)and ivory(712); 72cm(28 3/4")moss green cotton tape 2.5cm (1")-wide

The right bag; 90cm by 35cm(36"×14")cream quilting; 90cm by 10cm(36"×4")red check cotton; 40cm by 10cm(16"×4")white(1)Aida Cloth; DMC six-strand embroidery floss No. 25: a little each of light blue(334), grayish-green(503), red(817), white, yellowish brown(435)and cream(445); 72cm(28 3/4") white cotton tape 2. 5cm(1")-wide

Finished size: 37cm by 31cm(14 3/4"×12 3/8")
Instructions(same for the left and right):
1. Sew the embroiderd fabric to the front.
2. Sew the top pieces to the front and the back. Match the front and the back, with right sides facing. Sew both sides and the bottom, and turn over.
3. Turn over the top. Turn back the seam allowances inserting the cotton tapes, and baste. Topstitch along the verge with a sewing machine.
4. Fasten cotton tapes to the bag with 6-strand embroidery floss.

Add 1cm(3/8")seam allowances unless otherwise specified.
Finish the edges with a zigzag sewing machine.

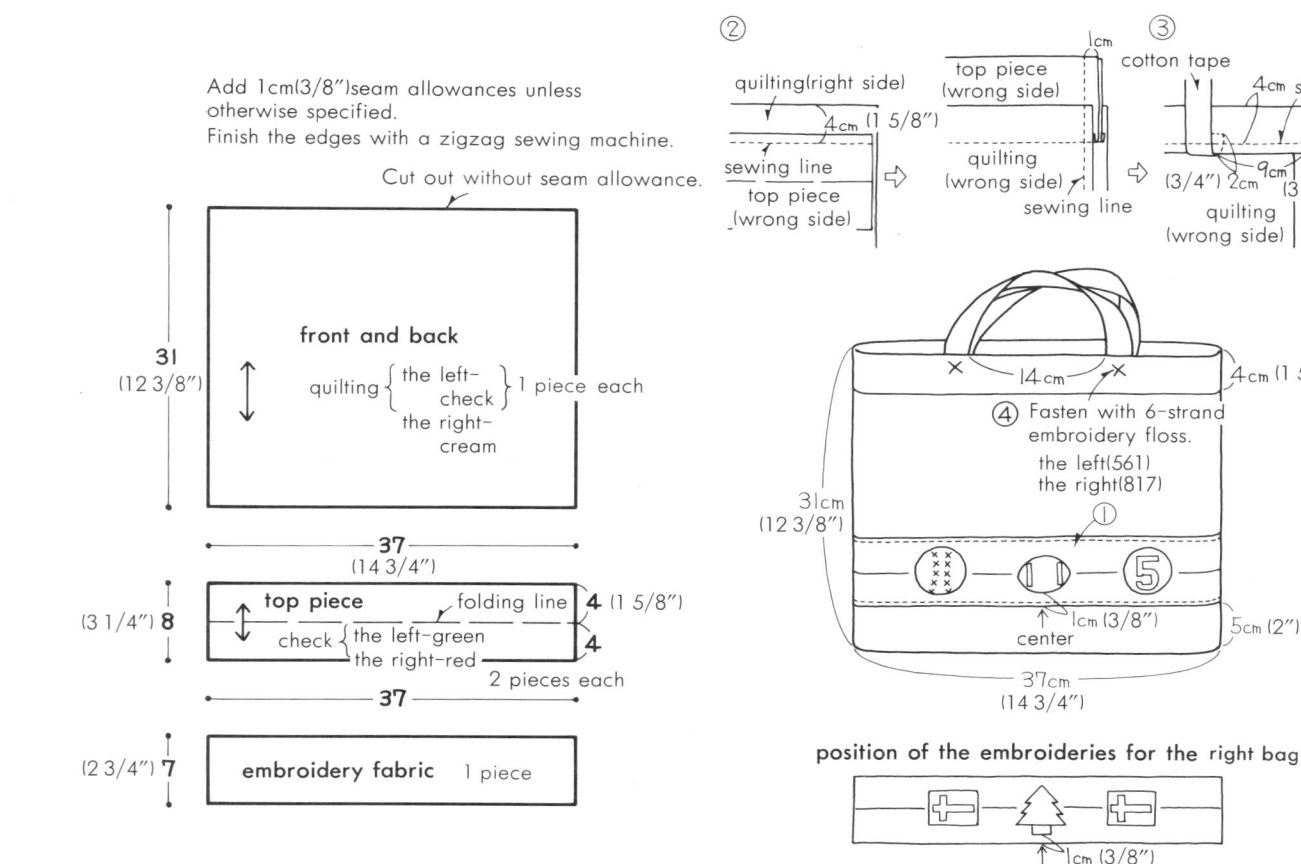

Cut out without seam allowance.

front and back
quilting { the left—check, the right—cream } 1 piece each
31 (12 3/8") × 37 (14 3/4")

top piece
folding line
check { the left—green, the right—red }
2 pieces each
8 (3 1/4") × 37, 4 (1 5/8") + 4

embroidery fabric 1 piece
7 (2 3/4")

② quilting(right side) / sewing line / top piece (wrong side) — 4cm (1 5/8")

top piece (wrong side) / quilting (wrong side) / sewing line — 1cm

③ cotton tape / 4cm sewing line / (3/4") 2cm (3 5/8") 9cm / quilting (wrong side)

④ Fasten with 6-strand embroidery floss.
the left(561)
the right(817)

14cm
4cm (1 5/8")
31cm (12 3/8")
1cm (3/8") center
5cm (2")
37cm (14 3/4")

position of the embroideries for the right bag
1cm (3/8")
center

3-strand   **the left bag**
(817) (745) (561) (300) (300) (300) (561) (950)
(712) (712)
center

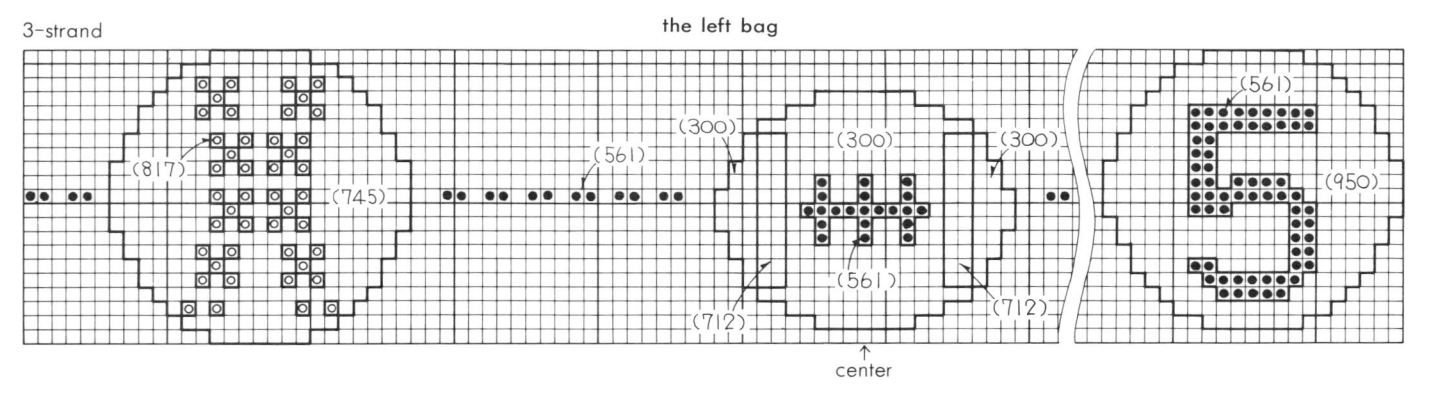

3-strand   **the right bag**
left flag(334) / right flag(817)
left flag(445) / right flag white
(435) (817) (503) (435)
center

61

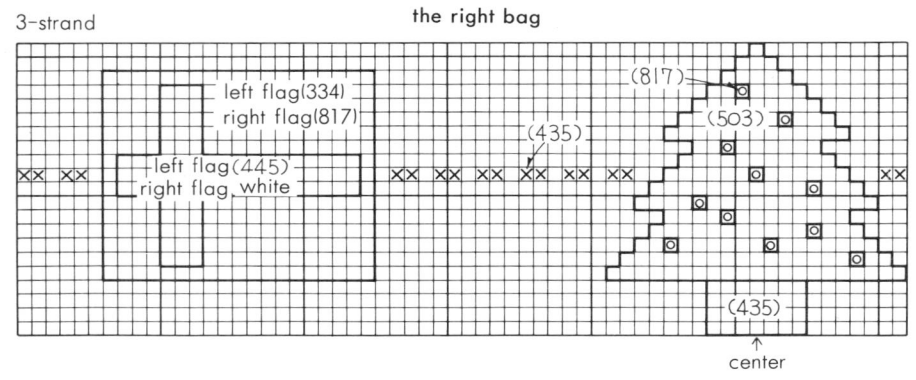

Gathered Skirt

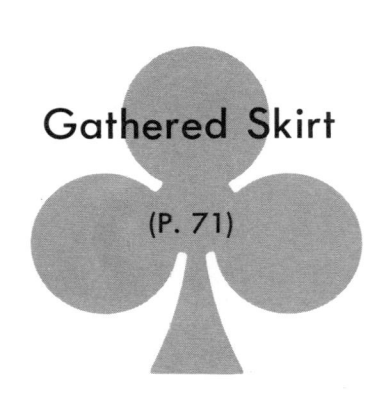

(P. 71)

Materials:
116cm(46 3/8")-wide by 80cm(32")check cotton viyella(lightly napped thin twill); 30cm by 18cm(12"×7 1/4")green Aida cloth; DMC six-strand embroidery floss No. 25: a little each of brown(300), dark brown(3371), red(817)and white; appropriate length of elastic of 0.7cm (1/4")-wide
Finished size: 32cm(12 3/4")in skirt length

Instructions:
1. Sew the top pieces to the embroidery fabric for pockets.
2. Match the center of the pockets and the patterns. Work design from a line 3.5cm(1 3/8")above the lower end of each pocket.
3. Sew both sides of the front and the back of the skirt together, with right sides facing, to make a loop. Sew the pockets to the skirt.
4. Make the elastic casing as in the figure. Turn back the hem twice and sew.
5. Pass 2 pieces of elastic through the casings one by one.

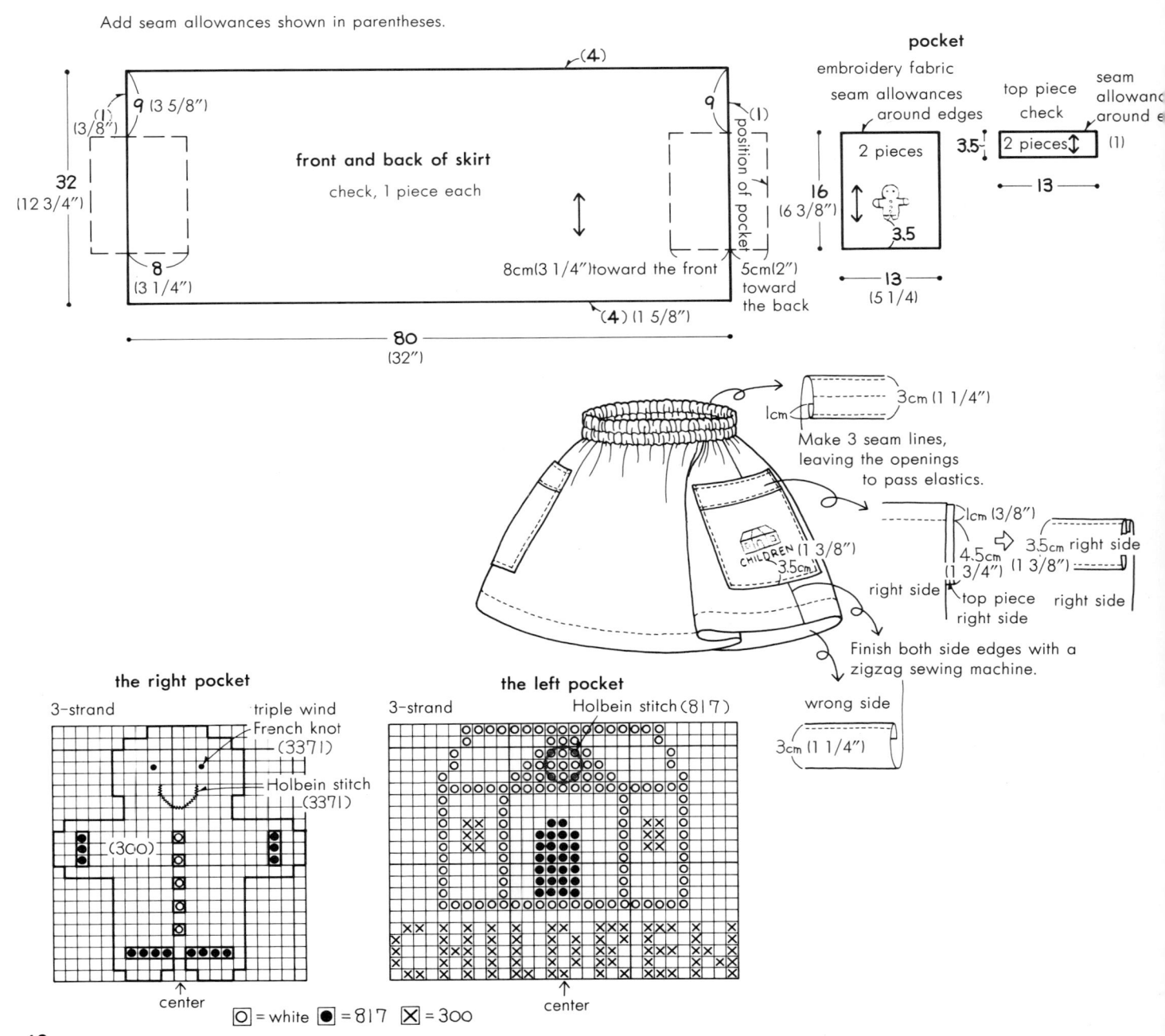

Add seam allowances shown in parentheses.

front and back of skirt — check, 1 piece each
32 (12 3/4") × 80 (32")
8cm(3 1/4")toward the front 5cm(2") toward the back
9 (3 5/8") 8 (3 1/4") (4)(1 5/8") (1)(3/8") (4)
position of pocket

pocket
embroidery fabric — seam allowances around edges — 2 pieces
16 (6 3/8") × 13 (5 1/4")
3.5
top piece check — 2 pieces — 3.5 × 13 (1)
seam allowance around edges

Make 3 seam lines, leaving the openings to pass elastics.
3cm (1 1/4") 1cm
1cm (3/8") 4.5cm (1 3/4") 3.5cm (1 3/8")
right side top piece right side right side
Finish both side edges with a zigzag sewing machine.
wrong side
3cm (1 1/4")

the right pocket 3-strand
triple wind French knot (3371)
Holbein stitch (3371)
(300)
center

the left pocket 3-strand
Holbein stitch (817)
center

◯ = white ● = 817 ✕ = 300

Shoe Tote (P. 72)

Materials:
The upper tote: 25cm by 52cm (10"×20 3/4") blue gray thick sheeting; 36cm by 52cm (14 3/8"×20 3/4") light blue gingham; 10cm (4") square white Aida cloth; DMC six-strand embroidery floss No. 25: a little each of light beige (822), brown (300), black (310) and moss green (561); 24cm by 2.5cm (9 5/8"×1") thin quilt foundation

The lower tote: 25cm by 52cm (10"×20 3/4") pink thick sheeting; 36cm by 52cm (14 3/8"×20 3/4") pink gingham; 10cm (4") square white Aida cloth, DMC six-strand embroidery floss No. 25: a little each of red (817), reddish brown (355), moss green (561) and blue (792); 24cm by 2.5cm (9 5/8"×1") thin quilt foundation

Finished size: See the figure.

Instructions (same for both tote):
1. After turning back seam allowances, sew the upper end and both sides of the embroidered fabric to the front of the outer bag fabric.
2. After turning back seam allowances, sew the top pieces and a bottom patch to the outer bag fabric.
3. Make a strap and a loop. Match the outer fabric and the lining with right sides facing. Insert the strap to the front and the loop to the back as in the figure. Sew the upper and the lower ends.
4. Open out the outer fabric and the lining, and fold them with top edges facing, as in the figure. Sew both sides, leaving a turning slit in the lining. Turn over, and stitch the turning slit. Put the lining within the outer fabric.

Add 1cm (3/8") seam allowances.

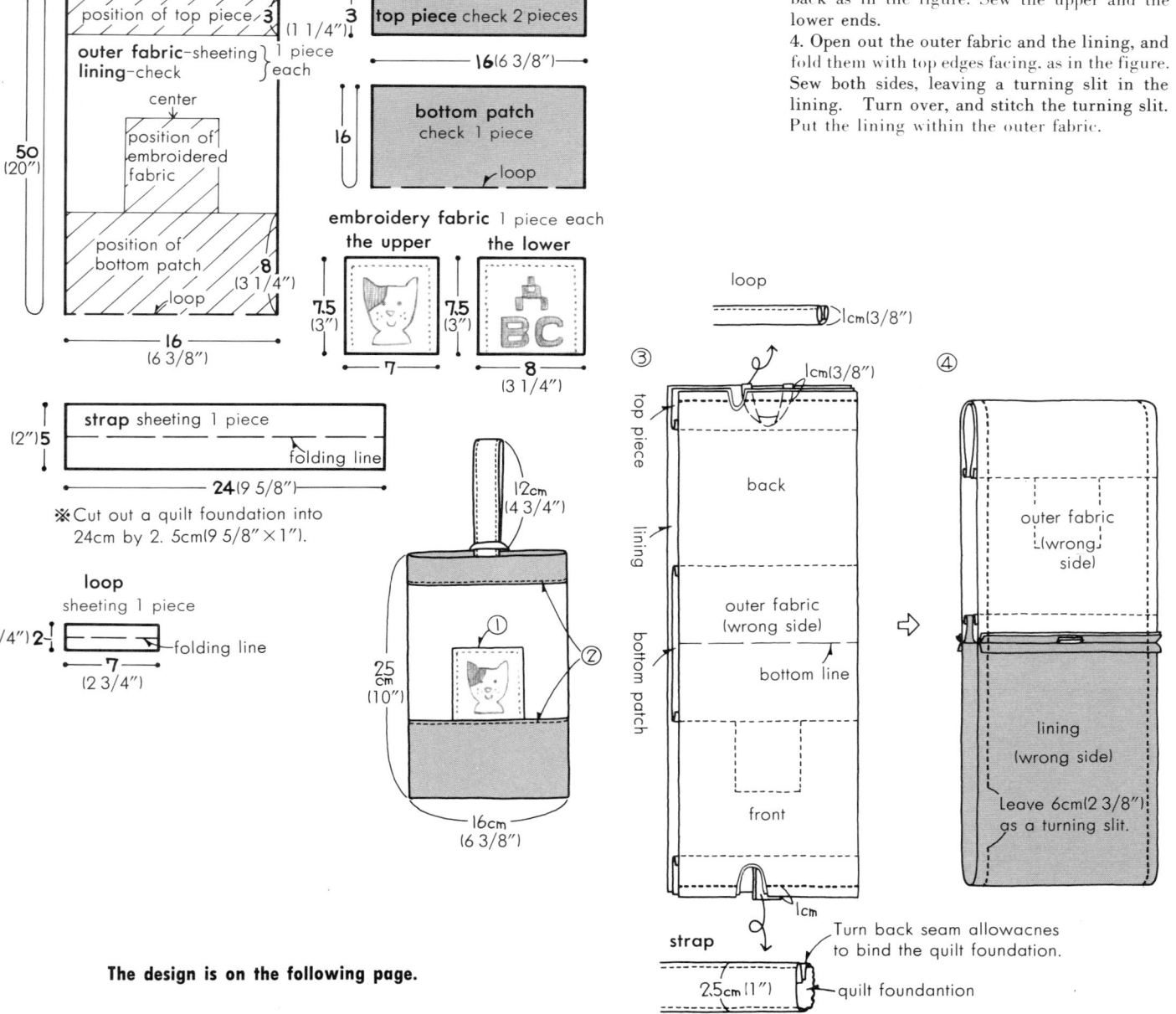

※Cut out a quilt foundation into 24cm by 2.5cm (9 5/8"×1").

The design is on the following page.

the upper tote
3-strand

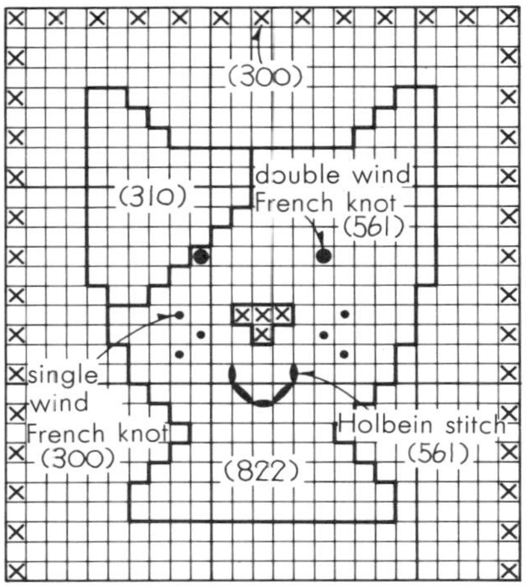

- (300)
- double wind French knot (561)
- (310)
- single wind French knot (300)
- (822)
- Holbein stitch (561)

the lower tote
3-strand

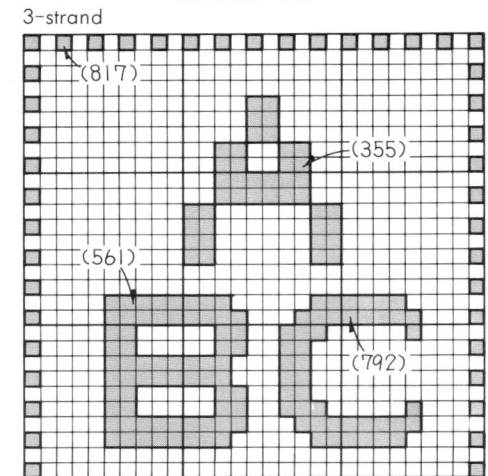

- (817)
- (355)
- (561)
- (792)

☆ Stitches used in this book ☆

Cross stitch

to stitch a cross
3 2 in
1 out 4

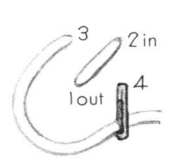

to work diagonally 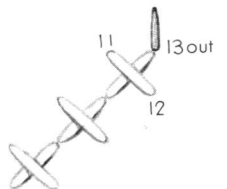
11   13 out
12
complete each cross

to work horizontally
2 in 4   6 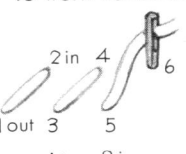
1 out 3   5
10   8 in
11   9   7 out
complete all crosses at returning; after working diagonal stitches from one end to the other, return to complete crosses.

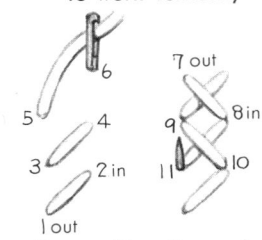

to work vertically
6   7 out
5   4   8 in
3   2 in 9
1 out   11 10

Holbein stitch

Staircase line
1 2 3 4 5 6
out in
10 9 8 7
in out

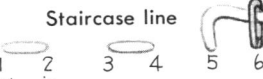

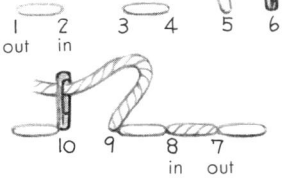

Straight line
1 out
3 2 in
4
9
7 out 10
8 in

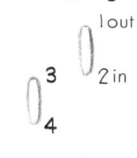

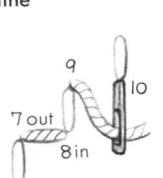

Straight stitch
1 out
2 in

1 3
2 4

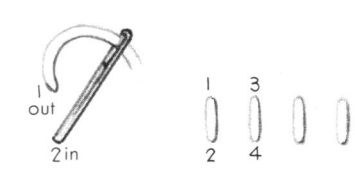

Running stitch
4 3 2 1
in out

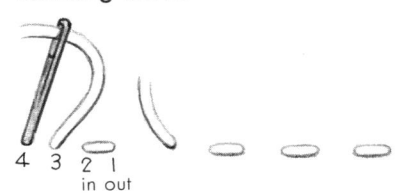

French knot (double winds)
Wind floss around a needle twice.
1 out
2 in
Place the needle at the base of the floss and stick vertically into fabric.

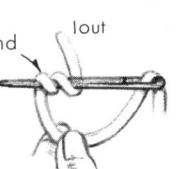

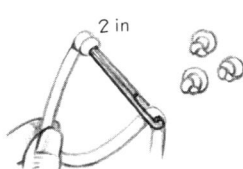

Outline stitch
3 5 4
2 in
1 out

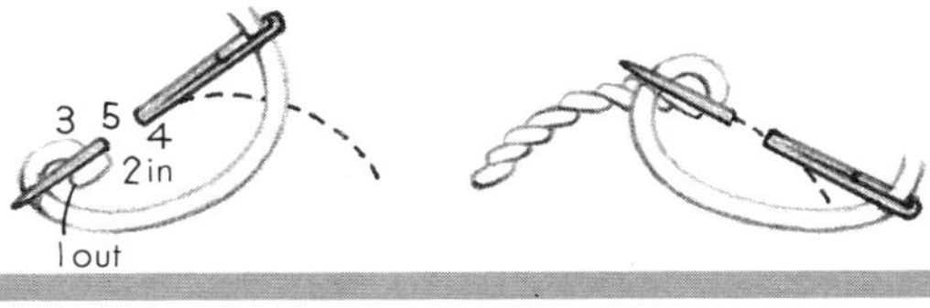

Fly stitch
1 out 2 in
3 out
1 2
3
4

Kids Land
Tricycle, Gingerbread Man, ABC, Football, Doll...
Instructions on page 45. Use Aida cloth.

Now I Know My ABC's. *Instructions on page 26. Use Aida cloth.*

68

season

Which Is Your Favorite Season?

Instructions on page 27. Use Use Aida cloth.

69

I Can Brush My Teeth All By Myself.

Instructions on page 46. Use Aida cloth.

Gathered Skirt, Lesson Bag

From mother to child-handmade items to cherish.
One point cross stitches take little time to make.
Instructions on pages 60~62.

Shoe Tote

The first day of school calls for a play shoe tote bag made by mom. Instructions on page 63.

72